In Full Flow

In Full Flow

Poetry

Rachel Heaney

Portal of Bliss

* * *

Dedicated to those who played a part,
In inspiring me with this poetic art...
Also, to those who may feel alone,
Searching for that place that feels like home...
As you take time out to start reading this,
Take a breath, tune in and feel the bliss...
This book is fully infused with love and healing,
May you feel the words and what they are revealing...

Contents

Contents

Contents

Contents

Contents

Contents

Contents

Contents

Contents

Contents

Contents

Contents

Contents

Contents

Contents

Contents

Contents

Missing Peace

There was a part of me missing, it had been missing for so long,
I'm not even sure what it was, or even where it may belong...
Maybe it was not missing at all,
Maybe I had just heard its call...
Maybe it was just hiding deep inside,
It had found a secret place to reside...
But I needed it to come out and play,
To come join me, and brighten up my day...
It was the light in moments of pain,
It was forgiveness instead of blame...
It was an open heart in the dark night,
It was the peace to end any fight...
It was the love I always knew was there,
But without it I felt so bare...
Raw and exposed wanting to hide,
But what I really wanted was love by my side...
The love in me didn't want to hide,
It wanted to walk with love in its stride,
It wanted to feel the peace in every day,
And not be affected by what others have to say...

Healing Heart

My heart hurt and longed to be free,
It was something I didn't want anyone to see...
There was a deep pain I held inside,
But no longer did it want to hide...
The protection shield needed to go,
So I could continue to evolve and grow...
Sometimes the hardest thing to do,
Is to deeply feel what is true...
To be seen in it all,
And be held when I fall...

Waves Of Emotion

As I looked out to the deep blue sea,
I felt the emotions that pulled at me...
They were dragging me under,
I couldn't stay afloat any longer...
So I surrendered and let go,
And allowed the waves to flow...
The deeper down I was swept,
The more peace that was met...

Held, Yet Also Free

Dancing in the breeze,
Hearing the birds in the trees...
I allow nature to move me,
Feeling held yet also free...
It is such music to my ears,
Bringing gratitude of tears...
There's no place I'd rather be,
Than when I have nature holding me...

Nourish My Soul

Dancing in the new day,
Listening to what the waves say...
My bare feet on the sand,
Feeling connected to the land...
Allowing the sunshine to fill me up,
One of the ways I like to fill my cup...
Allowing the sun to nourish my soul,
Freedom in every moment is my goal...

Senses Awakening

Immersed in my favourite meditation place,
I feel deeply held in this sacred space...
Nature dances through me,
So much beauty I can see...
Hearing the waves of the ocean roll by,
As the sun paints a golden sky...
I feel the softness of the breeze on my skin,
As I allow my senses to take it all in...

The Process Of Release

I listen to the birds in the trees,
As I feel the morning breeze...
There is something that wants to come through,
Maybe it's a message for me or for you...
Curling, twirling,
Unravelling, transforming...
The fears that disappear,
When you allow them near...
Allowing the old layers to peel,
And for that you need to feel...
Feel the pains from the past,
So no longer they will last...
If you really want to transform,
Ask yourself why do you conform...
Conform to rules set by who,
Do they really feel true...
Or are these rules just holding you back,
Keeping you imprisoned and off track...
Trust in this process of release,
Then you'll feel the waves of peace...

Soul To Soul Message

I'm not here to make you believe,
I'm just here to help you receive...
You have so many gifts deep inside,
No longer do they have to hide...
I'm here to help you remember why you're here,
Any energy densities I will help you clear...
Just receive the energy that comes through,
It's a soul-to-soul message from me to you...

Trusted Flow

The whispers of change in my ear,
I'm reminded there is nothing to fear...
When I trust in the divine flow,
There is nothing I need to know...
Guided so clearly to where I'm meant to be,
The new path always opens so effortlessly...

{ **10** }

Excitement Of Change

There was a time when I didn't like change,
I was struck with anxiety as things rearranged...
Faced with something that I didn't know,
I wasn't able to surrender and let go...
I'd work myself up into so much fear,
Now when I feel that change is near...
I feel the excitement deep within,
And await the new chapter to begin...

You Light Me Up

The portal was open & I was in flow,
I had nowhere to be & nowhere to go...
Guided to my mermaid place,
I felt the energy of your sweet embrace...
I jumped on your live to see what it was about,
You light me up is what I wanted to scream and shout...
However, I've felt a block in me to not speak,
I now realise that is just cowardly and weak...
I am open and loving and nothing else flows,
Even with all the rejection blows...
I want you to know that I am here,
And there is nothing you need to fear...
We signed up for this long before birth,
And agreed to meet here on Earth...
You trigger in me what I want to hide,
And vice versa, lets swallow our pride...
Let's 'let go' of fear and come back to love,
Is the message being sent from above...
I am you and you are me,
And with self-love that is intimacy...

Heart Clearing

My heart is almost clear,
It's been about a year...
Our souls have known all along,
Life has been tuning our soul song...
I'm keeping my heart open to you,
This is the 'one' love that is true...
I know you know this deep within,
Can you allow the next chapter to begin...
I'm going to give you space in the 3D,
But please keep sending signs to me...
So many you've already sent today,
Keep them coming, I love to play...
We're always together in the 5D,
I hope one day you finally see...

Time To Shine

I woke with a feeling it was time,
Time for me to really shine...
So I knew what it was I had to do,
I had to be brave and unfollow you...
Your posts are just a distraction to me,
And I get frustrated that you can't see...
You can't see the truth of why we met,
It was the divine plan that we help set...
Can we endure the same hurt & pain,
And then still choose for it to remain...
Or can we let the fear melt away,
And know what is really at play...
It's a divine union of you and me,
We're already one but your human can't see...
My superpower is my intuition,
It's what helped me with the recognition...
I knew it was you from the start,
Because you've always lived in my heart...

Energetic Touch

I receive your messages so much,
I feel your energetic touch...
This bliss that runs through me,
More powerful than eyes can see...
I did a oneness meditation,
It was our union in consecration...
We were at Whale Beach headland,
Looking out over clear water & sand...
It was our divine union,
A beautiful soul reunion...
We let go of any of the fears,
And just like that they disappeared...
We were both filled with light,
It will guide us through any night...
Our love radiates out to all,
No longer do we need to fall...
We just surrender into the sweet embrace,
And feel held in full bliss & grace...

The Perfect Trigger

I'm triggered, yes, I have work to do,
The fear of my fear coming true...
I'm having to sit in this pain,
So it will no longer remain...
And is it even necessary at all,
Or did my wounded self just fall...
I wasn't in a space of love,
So I was tested from above...
But if he is happy then so am I,
So maybe I'm meant to be with another guy...
Or is that just me wanting to hide,
Embarrassed that I've lost my pride...
Has he really chosen a friend over me,
The perfect trigger to set my heart free...
But I trust this divine plan,
I deeply know he is my man...
I just have some more triggers to sit in,
Before our physical union can begin...

Souls Longing To Meld

We entered into our portal of bliss,
Where we embraced with a passionate kiss...
Our energies merging as one,
And it's only just begun...
So much healing has taken place,
For us to merge with such grace...
This divine love and sacred union,
Has spent lifetime's brewing...
I love and trust you,
Do what you've got to do...
This love is so real,
We help each other heal...
Our love is out of this world,
And our souls long to meld...
To be together as one,
In spirit form it's already done...
Spirit will have us see each other,
But only after you've cleared with your mother...

Divine Conduit

The codes are coming in more,
Spirit is here knocking on my door...
And I'm ready to open up my channel full time,
To open up to receive messages from the divine...

Past Life Gifts

My past life gifts coming online,
Activations sent from the Divine...
Finally feeling freedom & fluidity,
As I remember my divinity...
Remembering why I came to Earth,
I volunteered to help in this rebirth...
Birthing a new age,
Ridding Earth of any rage...
Not Earth itself, but the collective,
Where I go is very selective...
Selected not by me,
But my guides no one can see...
There's always the deep knowing inside,
It's just allowing the mind to step aside...
I allow the Divine to be my guide,
The Divine's wishes are what I abide...
I'm sent to different places to be,
Where there is wisdom for me...
Or maybe I'm sent to clear the energy,
So the humans can be feeling free...
I transmute the density before I arrive,
It's part of my soul medicine in this life...

In Full Flow

Because if some people were to see,
They'd think I'd lost the plot mentally...
Like the Jester, I'm under cover,
Even to my twin lover...
He doesn't see who I am at my core,
So all the synchronicities he tries to ignore...
I was always working for my King,
To clear the block, I must sing...
My mermaid self will help him remember,
Before the 21st of December...
My beloved please notice the signs I send you,
This is the greatest love, it's true...
As you awaken to this divine union,
We'll be strongly guided to physical reunion...
Just keep following the signs to me,
I'm hearing them say 'meet at the tree'...
In the spiritual or physical I'm not yet sure,
But either way I'll be waiting at that door...
We agreed to this & knew one would awaken first,
My longing for you to remember is a strong thirst...
But patiently I wait for you,
All worth it for this love so true...

Longing For Home

The balance of yin and yang,
The spark from the big bang...
I am him & he is me,
But it's sometimes hard to see...
I am manifestation incarnation,
I am a visionary of creation...
Split in two we were longing for home,
For many lifetimes we would roam...
Searching in everything outside,
But we'd found the perfect place to hide...
We were deep within the entire time,
Just having to follow every sign...

Follow The Call

Where am I to be?
Where am I to go?
I need to be in full flow,
That is something I know...
What helps raise my vibration,
The sunshine, nature & the ocean...
When I am able to flow,
Spirit guides me where to go...
The freedom to follow the call,
Is what has me stand tall...
The sparkle in my eyes,
Cannot be disguised...
But I must do what I love,
Is the message from above...

Somewhere New

Maybe this is where I'm meant to be,
But can I live here and still feel free...
Would I be off going somewhere new,
Or would that not feel aligned or true...
What is it about March next year,
Is that when I'll have a change of career...
I'm feeling guided to get plenty of rest,
Is this the place or is it a test...
Am I meant to do this treatment of sound,
Or does it make me feel completely bound...
When I love everything free flow,
Will this not allow me to grow...
Or is there just a fear in me,
One that I can't quite see...

Dear Beloved

You show me how far I've come,
And without you it couldn't be done...
We've always been together as souls,
Together we signed up for these roles...
Nothing else matters when I understand that piece,
Because instantly I am filled with peace...
I feel our human journey together is done,
I can't admit that it's all been fun...
I'm always going to love you dear,
Now there is just nothing to fear...
I can still be me and you be you,
That is all I know to be true...
Forever you and me,
Even if you can't yet see...
I trust this process to the end,
Until then, messages of love I'll send...

White Buffalo Woman

You came to me at the perfect time,
The message you bring is so divine...
I never knew you before just now,
Not sure how I'd missed you somehow...
But I trust in you,
As you appear out of the blue...
I'm ready for your Keycode#7,
Please, I'm ready to be aligned with heaven...
I'm ready to be a Starseed Leading Light,
Spreading peace, no one has to fight...
How can I best share these gifts,
For the planet I'm ready to uplift...
If it's words you want me to say,
Or is it light language everyday...
Do I do online transmissions,
Igniting everyone's passions...
Codes, massage, dance, oils & love,
Is the message I'm getting from above...

Road Trip Pilgrimage

On the road in full flow,
Spirit guides me where to go...
If its north or south, east or west,
I just go & spirit organises the rest...
In full service to humanity,
Helping to assist with global unity...
Life becomes a full-time vision quest,
So easily & quickly things manifest...
In full alignment in every way,
When I listen to what spirit has to say...

Together Even If Apart

It's been a month since we spoke,
I laugh sometimes at this cosmic joke...
You help me so much on this journey,
In ways you'll probably never see...
Together even if we are apart,
We've been connected from the start...
I love you and I love me,
All while still feeling free...
Thank you for all the signs you send me,
They light me up so effortlessly...

Remembrance Deep Within

Being guided to places I had never been,
Seeing magical sites I had never seen...
It became clear this trip was so much more,
Than just finding magical places to explore...
There were certain places that held messages for me,
Not just messages that the eyes can see...
It was a remembrance deep within,
As I allowed this next chapter to begin...
The times I decided to look at a map,
Were the times that I was guided off track...
My greatest gift is my intuition,
It is the key that starts my ignition...
Guiding me to where I'm meant to be,
I cross paths with who I'm meant to see...
The reason is one the mind can't always know,
So I'm reminded to always trust and to always flow...
For me the flow is why I'm here,
Each day this gets even more clear...

Connecting To Self

Sometimes all that's needed is some time & space alone,
This can be challenging as the mind likes to roam...
It can also be the most rewarding time,
Connecting to self and to the divine...
Can you allow any emotions to flow,
Trusting there is nothing you need to know...
Or do you seek another to validate self-worth,
Stopping the process of your divine rebirth...
This was a long and winding journey for me,
It took me so many lessons to finally see...
Now I'm passionate to help others break through,
To live a life of love that is true...

Lesson #527

It was a prediction,
I knew before I knew...
I just hoped it wasn't true,
But it's here for me too...
This lesson known as life,
Has me feeling all kinds of strife...
I'm feeling so conflicted,
Did I allow myself to be restricted...
There are lessons here for me,
So many that I'm able to see...
When did it stop feeling aligned,
If only I could just rewind...
And in that moment choose to flow,
Going where I was guided to go...

Mirror Of Love

I am you & you are me,
The mirror is so clear to see...
Cycles and lessons help us grow,
But deep within we always know...
We are love in its purest form,
When the layers peel, we are reborn...
When fear melts away,
There is only love at play...
Just trust in the flow,
Let the mind chatter go...

Hold Your Light

When someone triggers you,
Do you use it to breakthrough...
Or maybe you succumb to a fight,
But can you instead hold your light...
Not giving your power away,
Being affected by what others say...
Can you own your trigger within,
And allow the deep healing to begin...
Or do you struggle and project,
What is it you want to protect...

Soul Mission

Can you act on your vision,
Can you trust in the flow...
We all have a soul mission,
Guiding us where to go...
When we surrender to the unknown,
The pathway is always shown...

Let Life Flow

Press clear on the mind,
Never hitting rewind...
When I surrender completely,
I feel it so deeply...
Embraced by waves of bliss,
I feel the delicious kiss...
Of energy running through me,
It's so good to just be...
Right here and right now,
It's to you that I bow...
This exact moment in time,
Is always perfect and divine...
When we just surrender and let go,
Life begins to magically flow...

Deep Knowing In Our Core

Be the calm amongst the storm,
As humanity is being reborn...
There is nothing we can trust more,
Than the deep knowing in our core...
Guiding us where to go,
Living life in constant flow...
When you deeply trust within,
Is when your soul mission will begin...

Heal & Renew

Life is all a balancing act,
What our minds think, we attract...
So, if life is feeling a little unstable,
Is there a thought you need to disable...
Remember to put your bare feet on the ground,
Through Mother Nature the answers can be found...
Take some time off just for you,
Allowing your body to heal and renew...
When you get that balance right,
Your soul will shine so bright...

Come Back To Now

Can you surrender to the peace within,
Not allowing the mind chatter to begin...
Or do you allow it to dictate your pain,
Creating a story making you insane...
Your mind might not want to sit in ice,
But what if the story you created was nice...
Soaking up the sunshine of this day,
Rewriting what the mind might try to say...
Or even better, come back to the now,
And all else will fade away somehow...

Stillness Sessions

Stillness Sessions are a vibe,
Where you'll find a loving tribe...
All drawn to the same one place,
Each week meeting a friendly new face...
Aligned with who you're meant to meet,
Early mornings have never been so sweet...
Some people come to receive a hug,
And others come to tune in and unplug...
To connect, to breathe and switch off the mind,
In stillness all the answers they can find...
Getting to experience a state of bliss,
Part of the week people don't want to miss...
Setting them up for the week to come,
While enjoying themselves and having some fun...
When you can surrender to the peace within,
It will allow your inner guidance to begin...

There Is No Limit

Everything you are seeking is already within you,
All the beauty you see is your reflection, it's true...
What you think you don't know, you already know,
There is no limit to how deep you can go...
So tune in and go within,
Allow your life to truly begin...

{ 38 }

Free To Explore

There is nothing that excites me more,
Than when I'm in nature & free to explore...
The sunlight beaming through the trees,
Senses alive with the fresh air breeze...
My bare feet on the ground,
All the answers are easily found...

Community Stillness

You're held so safely in the space,
For whatever emotions you need to face...
Or whatever journey you need to take,
The container is held until you wake...
We have the perfect space for you,
To go within and find what's true...

Helping Others

The ways I fill my cup,
Is by doing what lights me up...
Following the path that is most aligned,
And holding space as others unwind...
To live my life in full flow,
Helping others to adapt and grow...
This is my mission and why I came,
Helping others to do the same...
To remember why they are here too,
Letting go of anything that isn't true...
To live a life of love,
Is the message from above...

The Inner Journey

Going within was always the way,
It doesn't matter what anyone might say...
The outer reflects what is within,
So allow the inner journey to begin...
Then you will truly see,
This is the path to set you free...
The triggers are the gateway to heal,
Allowing yourself to drop in and feel...
Feel the emotion that wants to be felt,
Surrendering as these triggers start to melt...

Trusting The Change

More layers to surrendering and letting go,
Dropping back into living in full flow...
Trusting the change in the air,
Even if it's feeling raw and bare...
Change can happen in the blink of an eye,
A redirection to what you align...
Energy is everything, it will never lie,
It is something that I just can't deny...
If something doesn't quite feel right,
Something you can't see with your sight...
But a feeling of something that isn't true,
Trust that feeling and honour you...
Take any lessons you need to learn,
And stand in your power and quietly turn...
Turn to face what feels true for you,
And trust these changes that came out of the blue...
They are a redirection,
A bit of a course correction...

{ **43** }

Grounded Flow

Staying grounded amongst the storm,
Has become somewhat of my new norm...
Things changing in the blink of an eye,
All part of the divine plan, I can't deny...
Each day I reach a new level of trust,
Surrendering to the change is a must...
Allowing everything to melt away,
Not being affected by what others say...
This is the greatest freedom of all,
Breaking down any limiting wall...
I'm staying grounded but in full flow,
Just when I thought I was about to go...
Life already had another plan for me,
Something that the eye can't yet see...
So I will be staying around a little longer,
Before I head off to explore and wander...

Lovingly Letting Go

This Scorpio full moon got me good,
Illuminating to me where I stood...
So much more than meets the eye,
The lessons and gifts I can't deny...
Diving deep into this death and rebirth,
Seeing so clearly what is ready to unearth...
The unconscious beliefs that were at play,
I now see so clearly what they had to say...
Now I can lovingly let them go,
So I can drop back into my flow...
True acceptance comes from within,
I'm excited for this next chapter to begin...

Leap Into The Unknown

That moment of being in the void,
Part of the leap I cannot avoid...
But the unknown excites me,
That leap before I can see...
The echoes of trust within myself,
What I'm here to teach everyone else...
Not knowing where I'm being guided to,
Doors always opening out of the blue...
I've been here many times before,
Reminding myself to trust deep in my core...
When I trust so deeply in my flow,
There is nothing else I need to know...
I just listen to my intuition,
It's the key that starts my ignition...
Soon I'll be hitting the road some more,
Finding new places to explore...
Sharing my gifts along the way,
Listening to what the whispers say...

Create The Spark

What wants to come through,
Is it a message for me or for you...
What am I being called to do,
What is it that really feels true...
To be a guiding light,
Which means I can't hide from sight...
People need to know where to go,
So they can live a life of flow...
My activations help create the spark,
Awakening them from the dark...
There is nothing I physically need to do,
It will all happen out of the blue...
I am a pillar of light,
Shining so very bright...
With a frequency that is felt,
It's one of the gifts I've been delt...

She

For too long she kept her gifts hidden from sight,
Not wanting to upset anyone by shining too bright...
But the time has come to share what's true,
She activates others to help them shine too...
Her presence has been doing it all along,
Helping others to awaken to their soul song...
She works in dimensions the mind can't fully understand,
Where she clears energy with the movement of her hand...
There was a time where she would have called this woo woo,
But now there is nothing else that feels more true...
She's here to help others to adapt and grow,
So she shares her gifts where she is guided to go...
She is me and possibly you too,
If so, please keep sharing what's true...

Third Eye Vision

When I close my eyes I see,
All the answers are within me...
Everything that I need to know,
All the places I need to go...
Visions flash in my mind,
All the truth I easily find...
The channel to the divine,
It's where I truly shine...

Wisdom Of The Tree

Just like the tree,
The wisdom is within me...
Standing strong in the ground,
All the nourishment can be found...
Plugged in and connected,
So guided and directed...
Take a moment to stop and be,
Observe and witness like a tree...
Nature has so much to teach us,
Just slow down, there is no rush...
You'll find messages everywhere you look,
Life becomes a magical story book...
You'll notice every little thing,
And all the messages that they bring...
Your intuition will become stronger,
And feelings of bliss will last longer...

What Wants To Bloom

Today is the Taurus New Moon,
What is it that wants to bloom...
When anything is possible, what would I do,
I'd continue to share my light, that is true...
Aligning with the people who are for me,
Bringing to light what they need to see...
I am the lighthouse, may I never forget,
Otherwise, I'll live a life of regret...

Magic Of Flow

The magic of being in flow,
There is nothing I need to know...
When I surrender into the bliss,
I unlock more of my inner gifts...
Doing what makes me shine,
And trusting in the divine...
I'm always where I'm meant to be,
When I listen to the wisdom within me...
This is available to all,
But many ignore the call...
If you feel those whispers within,
Allow the next chapter to begin...

Trust & Flow

Visions pop in my mind,
Like a puzzle of some kind...
I'm shown a place I need to be,
Not knowing who I'm going to see...
Or why I'm being sent to a certain place,
I just know to follow with ease and grace...
I know it will make sense when I go,
A constant reminder to trust and flow...
The feeling inside,
I can't describe...
Doors will always open out of the blue,
When you trust the guidance inside of you...

Share What's True

In every moment we have a choice,
Do we run and hide or share our voice...
What is underneath the fear,
What is there still to clear...
The mind will sometimes get in the way,
Sneaky tricks it will try to play...
Can you lean into that edge and share what's true,
Feeling a sense of relief wash over you...

Hidden Behind The Mask

It was a soul journey that I was being guided to take,
There were many leaps of faith I had to make...
Burleigh is where I've spent most of these past seven years,
All the memories bringing gratitude filled tears...
Many friends I've met in this place,
Who continue to put a smile on my face...
June 2021 is different from those seven years ago,
Today there are many masks & people that may not know...
May not know that they have a choice,
They have an opportunity to use their voice...
Yet they were hidden behind their mask,
Where's the common sense I wanted to ask...
My heart was breaking for the fear they must feel,
I was just wanting them to know what is real...
But maybe what is true for them isn't true for me,
And what if what I know is something they can't yet see...
I wanted to help bring them more peace,
So I danced on the beach with my niece...
She had a song that she couldn't stop singing,
I loved the message these words were bringing...

*

RACHEL HEANEY

*

"Lately, I've been thinking,
I want you to be happier, I want you to be happier..."

*

We danced on the beach as the waves rolled in,
Those words we were continuing to joyfully sing...
Smiling at whoever walked by,
Seeing a smile reflect in their eye...
Reminding them that we hold them with love,
Channeling some healing vibes from above...

Sacred Union

This sacred union of the divine,
Is within me and is already mine...
The reflection from an outside source,
Is just the mirror of this inside course...
Always connected within,
Not waiting for union to begin...
Because I feel you with me now,
We exist in a different realm somehow...
At any moment I can go within,
And I feel my heart start to sing...
Your presence can be felt in many ways,
All I'll treasure it for the rest of my days...
Even if in the 3D we do not unite,
You'll always be helping me shine so bright...
You are me and I am you,
This is what I know to be true...
A reflection of each other,
Helping each other to discover...
These gifts that can be found,
When we close our eyes & feel the sound...
The sound is a vibration of you and me,
It's just something the eyes can't fully see...

{ 56 }

Boundaries

The week that has just been,
So much happening in the unseen...
Shocked by the energy coming my way,
But it was time for me to have my say...
No more will I allow people to dim my light,
I know I am here to shine so bright...
These lessons I have gone through,
Were things I deep down knew...
But I needed to share what was true,
I won't be abused out of the blue...
My inner masculine stepped up for me,
Sharing my voice so the others can see...
They may have thought I wasn't strong,
But wow, I definitely proved them wrong...
I now release the hold they had over me,
I'm the only one I can trust, I now see...

Sweet Little Stone

I sat amongst the rocks & shells,
And felt a feeling of angel bells...
Noticing all the beauty in every little thing,
Wondering what wisdom they would all bring...
Those rocks that were rough,
I wondered if they felt enough...
And what about that sweet little stone,
I wondered if it felt left out and alone...
And did that shell know it had a message to share,
Or did it just keep quiet thinking no one would care...
Although they were all different in size,
Their beauty they could not disguise...
Everyone had its own unique gift,
They all helped my sadness to uplift...
If ever you are having a tough day,
Tune into what your surroundings have to say...
There may be a lovely message you'll find,
And being present will take you out of your mind...

Nobody Was In The Wrong

Held by the man that I didn't want to see,
He held the safest space for me...
We uncovered what was really going on,
Knowing nobody was in the wrong...
We were the perfect duo for the dance,
And living with him was the perfect chance...
To bring to the surface what I needed to see,
To forgive all the things we couldn't both see...

Mystery Man

I saw you from a distance as I waited for my coffee at Nook,
You looked and felt so familiar from my very first look...
Have we met before,
My mind wanted to know more...
You said hi as I walked by,
But silly me went all shy...
I wanted to come back your way,
But I didn't know what to say...
Hopefully our paths will cross again,
I trust the mystery of where and when...

We Have A Choice

Ten years ago, the best thing I ever did for me,
Was turn off and stop watching the TV...
Everything on there was implanting fear in me,
I'd realised it wasn't something I wanted to see...
We don't know what we don't know,
And maybe we are all here to grow...
So many people are starting to awaken,
From their deep slumber they are shaken...
They start turning off the news which had them in fear,
They realise they have a choice what comes near...
Is it a hug from a loved one,
Or does the distance rule make them run...
Maybe they decide to ditch the mask,
What's the point they may finally ask...
They start to smile at everyone that walks by,
They see a glimmer of hope in the others eye...
And slowly but surely the love ripples out,
We have a choice they want to scream & shout...
But they know that it's a shock to abruptly awake,
So it's their intuition that guides the choices they make...
They start questioning within,
When did all these lies begin...

Love Or Fear

Every moment we can choose love or fear,
When we choose one, the other will disappear...
Neither is wrong or right,
Or any reason to fight...
We are all together on this Earth,
Experiencing this time of rebirth...
Seeing things from another point of view,
Will help you know what's true for you...

Times Of Change

The mirror of life staring back at you,
Look within to find what you always knew...
The truth is deep within your core,
Just tune in to find out more...
I know these times of change can be hard for some,
So many fears that may need to be overcome...
You may not know where to turn,
Or who can guide you as you unlearn...
If so, please know I am here for you,
To support you as you find what's true...

Gratitude For This Day

The sand beneath my bare feet,
The sunrise that my eyes got to meet...
The sunshine on my skin,
The people that make me grin...
Puppy cuddles with little Jacks,
Beautiful nature walking tracks...
The people who I passed by,
Those that smiled and said hi...
The hugs from those I love,
The guidance from above...
Aligning me where I'm meant to be,
I am grateful for the love I feel within me...

8/8 Portal

Guided to my meditation rock,
There were codes waiting to unlock...
I just had to drop into my flow,
Then all the codes would show...
Coming rapidly through my hands,
Not something the human mind understands...
But the transmission was strong,
We are always where we belong...
There is always a place I feel so free,
And that place is constantly within me...
Activations to ignite others in their portal,
Reminding them their souls are immortal...

{ 65 }

Open Mind

We all have a choice to live with an open mind,
We also have a choice to stay closed off and blind...
Neither is right or wrong,
Either way, we all still belong...
We belong to ourselves and no other,
Not our father, mother or our lover...
Everything comes back to the self,
Within, you will find an abundance of wealth...
So before you seek someone for advice,
Ask yourself, do I need to think twice...
We have all the answers hidden inside,
No longer do they want to hide...
When we realise everything comes from within,
That is when true freedom will begin...

The Experience

Can you surrender to the peace within,
Not allowing the mind chatter to begin...
Or do you allow it to dictate your pain,
Creating a story that wants to remain...
Your mind might not want to sit in ice,
But what if the story you created was nice...
Soaking up the sunshine of this day,
Rewriting what the mind might try to say...
Even better, just come back to the now,
And all the stories will fade away somehow...
You are held so safely in the space,
For whatever emotions you need to face...
We have the perfect event for you,
To go within and find what's true...
If this is a journey you want to take,
The final decision is yours to make...

Reflection Of You

Mirror mirror, what do you see,
I see the reflection staring back at me...
If there is ever a doubt in my mind,
When I look at you, the answers I find...
And if there is something I can't yet see,
You reflect it back so beautifully...
The mirror is me and also you,
Illuminating a depth of love so true...

Follow Your Bliss

Always trusting, always flowing,
Guided by my inner knowing...
Many paths we can choose to take,
With different choices we have to make...
What path is most aligned for you,
Deep down you know what is true...
When we follow our bliss,
The path we will not miss...

I Choose You!

It's true,
I choose you...
Not just today,
But every day...
I'm sorry it's taken so long,
For me to find out where I truly belong...
Wrapped up in your arms is where I want to be,
Not swept away by all the distractions I see...
When I look into your eyes,
I see that you're me in disguise...
So, if I really love me,
You are the reflection that I see...
There is a fear that you won't choose me back,
But that is just a story keeping me off track...
I know we have similar pains from the past,
But no longer do they have to last...
I'm excited for all the adventure & fun,
We get to enjoy now the hard work is done...

Feeling The Flow

Never have I felt so free,
Diving into the clear blue sea...
The light from the sun shining through,
Dolphins appearing out of the blue...
A connection I cannot describe,
Surrounded by water is my vibe...
Having the most relaxing week out at sea,
As we sailed off, I felt the bliss wash over me...
Soaking up the sun rays,
Feeling the flow of the waves...
There's no place I'd rather be,
Than when I have water surrounding me...

Synchronicities Of Life

I laugh at the synchronicities of life,
Like running into him & his possible future wife...
I could feel he was trying to walk by,
He didn't want to have to say hi...
But I got the attention of his girl,
So the awkwardness had to unfurl...
She was stunning in every way,
A beautiful couple I have to say...
After all that I've been journeying through,
I now see what deep down I always knew...
He was never going to choose me,
It kept my story safe I now see...
Running into him was a blessing in disguise,
Showing me the same pattern with other guys...
I don't ever want to be someone's second choice,
So, if I feel a connection, I need to use my voice...
If in that moment I can't be met,
That is not where my energy will be set...
I'll flow and be open for my true King,
So wherever you are, I'm calling you in...

Depths Of You & Me

There has always been something at my core,
Telling me there is so much to explore...
Just dive into the unknown,
All the beauty will be shown...
I'm not just talking about the deep blue sea,
I'm talking about the depths of you and me...
We all have so much beauty to see,
And it all begins internally...

Lady Musgrave

The water is crystal clear,
Turtles swim up so near...
Bird life I've never seen,
The island is so serene...
Connected to the forest and the sea,
The energy ripples within me...

Great Awakening

They are being manipulated and have been from the start,
It's not something that's easy to realise and it breaks my heart...
When you realise you've lived a lie,
It's the moment your ego must die...
Let go of what you thought you knew,
Nothing they told you was ever true...
They needed you to believe what they said,
All the things they programmed into your head...
But it's time to ask yourself why you believe what they say,
Do you always just follow the crowd when they go a certain way...
Or do you trust what feels right for you,
Your inner guidance that always knew...
For so long I'd given my power away,
I just listened to what others had to say...
Then a remembrance sparked within,
And my great awakening did begin...
A powerful journey full of rewards,
I trust this poem has struck some chords...

Self-Love Is The Cure

To be truly free,
Is to be all of me...
If I love me,
What would I see...
I'd see love staring back at me,
The true gift of simplicity...
What is stopping the mirror from being pure,
No matter the question, self-love is the cure...

Release & Expansion

What if I truly released all the blame,
Fully letting go of any bits of shame...
The expansion would be next level,
I need to forgive the so-called devil...
He was actually the greatest gift to me,
He helped me to truly see...
All the pains I carried from the past,
They didn't want to remain or last...
Even though I thought he was my man,
The biggest shift happened when I ran...
But now I see what I was running from,
It had been a habit of mine for so long...
When that acceptance came from within,
It allowed the next chapter to begin...
Now I am ready to accept & rechoose,
All the synchronicities hold the clues...
I'm calling in sacred union,
The ultimate divine reunion...

Forgive Them All

When she decided to forgive them all,
All the stories began to fall...
And she started to believe in herself,
She realised she's more important that anyone else...
From the inside out she started glowing,
And her life was magically flowing...
Now if she had advice to pass on,
It would be to stay strong...
To forgive & believe in the self,
Know within is an abundance of wealth...
You'll find yourself in a state of flow,
Always being guided which way to go...
Just trust within,
Allow the next chapter to begin...

Beyond Time & Space

Sometimes I know without knowing how I know,
It always comes back to trusting in the flow...
There are also times where I may seem blind,
Where the mystery of life whispers in my mind...
Just accept the unexpected,
Present moment being respected...
Not in the mind remembering your download,
And trusting not a past vision you were showed...
Gratitude to be in pure presence,
Feeling his divine essence...
Whatever transpires in the now,
Escapes any thought form somehow...
Just energetic beings merging as one,
The deepest & most beautiful healing has begun...
Beyond time and space,
Held in his embrace...
Love in its most unconditional form,
A part of me being completely reborn...

Awakening From The Slumber

Are we ever truly fully awake,
A lifetime of conditioning we need to break...
But awake from what you may ask,
Everything that is hidden behind the mask...
Is it a mask for the eyes,
Or is it a full-face disguise...
People telling others to 'wake up',
But which way do you look at the cup...
Is it half full or half empty,
Different perspectives are a plenty...
Could we all just soften and open,
From the dream scape we have awoken...
Everything else becomes our own choice,
Not conditioned by the media voice...
We come to the deep peace inside of us,
Knowing we are the only ones we need to trust...
Suddenly we love what is,
What's hers is hers and what's his is his...

Self-Acceptance

We can choose to listen to our inner guidance,
Between heart, head & intuition is the dance...
When we trust in what comes through,
We don't always know how we knew...
Can you trust in yourself,
Ignoring the fears of everyone else...
What are your gifts hidden inside,
No longer do they want to hide...
I am good enough the voice whispered in my mind,
I remembered thinking how that voice was so kind...
Then suddenly another came into judge,
Giving the kindness a nasty budge...
Where did that judgement come from, I ask,
And I'm reminded that being human is my task...
I may not be perfect in the eyes of some,
But no longer do I need to run...
When I accept all of me,
It's a pure reflection I will see...

Unconditional Love

Family comes in many forms,
Not just the one that you were born...
We choose our birth Mum & Dad,
We take on any karmic baggage they had...
Maybe the things they didn't know how to heal,
Or maybe they were never taught how to feel...
You put your hand up to heal the karmic pain,
So for future generations it would not remain...
Maybe it created some tension,
As you paved the path of ascension...
Although you love them with all your heart,
You knew you needed to take some time apart...
The separation does not need to last forever,
Please know you are always together...
Connection does not have any rules at all,
It's unconditional love and it's always your call...

Phone Detox

Who am I without my phone,
It feels so foreign to me I've just been shown...
My phone won't switch on,
And I'm not sure what's wrong...
I feel this is a lesson for me,
To stop relying on something outside of me...
The phone is a gateway to many distractions,
Scrolling for hours getting lost in the captions...
I mainly use it to take a pic,
Keep it on flight mode is the trick...
This morning I couldn't even take the sunrise shot,
I realised I actually like to do that a lot...
I like to share it so others can see,
The way the sunrise greets us so beautifully...
But this morning I appreciated it just for me,
Allowing me to drop in and truly be...
As I sip on my coffee while soaking up this sun,
I feel the new level of presence that has begun...

Witnessed In It All

Do you allow yourself to be fully seen,
Some may ask what does that even mean...
To allow yourself to be witnessed in it all,
As all the layers gently start to fall...
Peeling away what barriers you'd put in place,
Allowing the other to hold you with an energetic embrace...
Feeling any discomfort that may arise,
Certain emotions may take you by surprise...
Noticing the times you want to run & hide,
Then embracing the courage you have deep inside...
Sitting with any of the emotional pain,
Knowing it no longer wants to remain...
In order to truly heal,
We must allow ourselves to feel...
With unconditional love reflected back to us,
We know we can let go and fully trust...
Always right where we belong,
Yet we may have been searching for so long...

Island Gifts

As we went off diving on this beautiful day,
My intuition was guiding me another way...
Swimming into the current I had to kick a little faster,
The fish I saw were getting larger and larger...
The sun was shining through the water to the sand,
As I arrived at a magical secluded island...
I honoured the many spirits of this place,
And asked if I could explore their space...
They told me there was something special for me,
And I'd know it as soon as I would see...
So I spent my time looking around,
But my gift I had not yet found...
I went into a cave & a song channeled through,
It wasn't a voice of someone I knew...
It was so angelic and had me in awe,
So I just kept singing more and more...
I didn't know the words I was singing,
But I felt the activation they were bringing...
Surrounding the cave was a cliff to climb,
In some places the rocks were ultra-fine...
At some stages I thought I was stuck,
Then a hand appeared to help me up...

In Full Flow

The view from the top was like nothing I'd ever seen,
The clearest turquoise waters and so serene...
As I climbed the edge keeping my eyes on the ground,
Another powerful gift I had just found...
At my feet lay a snake skin,
I love the message they bring...
Letting go of what serves you no more,
Peeling the layers to what's at your core...
It's also the kundalini rising,
It's a power there is no disguising...
I felt the energy coming through my bare feet from the land,
Engulfing my whole body and out through my hand...
I felt a shell call out to me,
The gift I'd know as soon as I'd see...
As I held this shell in my palm,
I felt a blissful wave of calm...
The shell was activating a remembrance in me,
I could feel something happening internally...
The messages were coming through stronger,
Until I couldn't stay awake any longer...

Merman

He did what he had to do,
Letting go of a love so true...
It didn't make much sense to the mind,
But he knew the answers he would find...
So he set off sailing on his own,
He had new places to roam...
Allowing the wind to guide the way,
He trusts the mystery in each day...
Guided to places he's never been,
Seeing sights he has never seen...
He takes people on trips to explore,
Showing them there is so much more...
He has the most beautiful soul,
Allowing others to let go of control...
From the first day sailing with him,
I saw so much beauty in everything...
All the subtleties in the things he'd do,
The many ways he'd look after the crew...
Whether it be a pillow to rest your head,
Or helping to set up a starlit bed...
His presence holds the ability to heal,
Any blocks he will help you reveal...

In Full Flow

He'll hold you in his loving embrace,
Allowing you to melt with such grace...
He is a real-life merman living at sea,
I'm so grateful for his amazing company...
He is brave, cautious and ultra-strong,
He can even freestyle you a song...
He is adventurous, handsome & so much fun,
He even knows how to use a spear fishing gun...
He'll dive to the depths with you in the caves,
And even loves to surf the reef waves...
He has a YouTube channel for you to see,
What life is like living so free...
Join him on the ocean,
As the sails set motion...
Bring your snorkel and fins,
Enjoy the magic the water brings...
The man I talk about on this page,
This divine masculine's name is Sage...

He

He is unlike anyone I've ever met,
But I knew him and we hadn't met yet...
We had both walked such similar paths,
Slowly we'd created so many masks...
About who we thought we were meant to be,
Not knowing what it was to be free...
Using many distractions to escape the mind,
Keeping us so stuck and so very blind...
What would it take to escape this pain,
Not wanting to go on if it was to remain...
Then he realised he had all the tools inside of him,
And that's when his life truly started to begin...
He found what he was passionate about,
So he started up community in the Mount...
Breathwork, meditation and beautiful connection,
He supported others on their journey of ascension...
Then he got the call to move overseas,
To facilitate on the beach as everyone breathes...
The space he holds is like no other,
So he created a business with his soul Brother...
The expansion and growth was ultra-quick,
Everyone wanted to know what's the secret trick...

In Full Flow

The secret is to find what you're passionate about,
But there is no need to scream & shout...
Because when you're embodied you don't need to preach,
What you do and who you be is how you teach...
He embodies so many amazing things,
And an energetic transmission he brings...
He really sees everyone for who they are,
His presence will melt through any past scar...
When I allowed myself to be truly seen,
By this divine masculine being...
The deepest healing occurred within,
Allowing me to really drop in...
Seeing the patterns that were at play,
Knowing I have a choice in every day...
He was the mirror for everything I couldn't yet see,
He was reflecting it back so perfectly...
He's my travel buddy, co-worker & best friend,
We're on a mission to help others to transcend...
This divine masculine's name is Ry,
He is the most amazing guy...
If you're blessed enough to cross paths with him,
You'll feel the shifts start occurring within...

Many Moons Ago

The vision I saw many moons ago,
I was shown where I had to go...
Airlie Beach was calling my name,
The Gold Coast I was not to remain...
So I road tripped up in full flow,
Trusting the guidance of where to go...
Now I sit here manifesting what I'm calling in,
I'm calling in sacred union to begin...
I'm also calling in time on boats,
Being in, on or under the water I love the most...
Calling in connection, love & so much more,
Calling in a beautiful community to adore...
If I'm meant to do my healings again,
I'll be shown the place of where & when...
Calling in a beautiful space to stay,
One where there is lots of fun and play...
Connection with the spirit of the land,
Let them channel healing through my hand...
The feeling of bliss always running through me,
All the beauty & love I will see...
Stillness sessions in a stunning space,
The energy flows with such ease & grace...

In Full Flow

Getting my feet planted on the Earth,
Allowing guidance in this great rebirth...
The feeling of being fully met by my man,
He is in full acceptance I live in a van...
He holds me allowing me to fully open,
My heart opens more with every word that is spoken...
He lights me up in every way,
Life with him brings so much play...
Trusting life and the mirror in front of me,
It's pure joy reflected back that I see...
Because I found that within myself,
It's now reflected by everyone else...

My Inner Reality

The happiness I feel is inside of me,
The sadness I feel is inside of me...
Everything in life that I see,
Is a reflection of my inner reality...
This place has Hawaii vibes,
Connecting me to many tribes...
And different land to drop in,
Allowing a sacred exchange within...
Is it safe for me to be on the land alone,
Or is it elsewhere I need to roam...
He will be away for a week,
Maybe I can make the space so sweet...
I can honour and tend to the land,
As I also tune into my brand...
I'll ask spirit what wants to come through,
Is it a message for me or for you...

Rhythm Of Life

Things are shifting before my eyes,
Peoples pain they cannot disguise...
What will it take for them to break the chain,
So these trauma bonds won't remain...
If everyone can come back to the now,
The turbulence will fade away somehow...
Move your bodies to the music,
What is it that you are choosing...
Dance with the rhythm of life,
It will always keep you out of strife...
We can manifest our dreams through dance,
Just move your body, give it a chance...

Stuck In A Safety Net

I asked spirit if they were happy for us to stay,
It seems like they are humorous & like to play...
Because as I went to drive my van out,
There were some things that I started to doubt...
Maybe I'm not meant to leave at all,
Maybe the spirit of the land made the call...
Letting me know I'm welcome on the land,
As my wheels got stuck in the dirt like sand...
He helped to dig & to set us free,
I love the safety he provides for me...
But what is it I can't see within,
That has me think that I need him...

Mermaid Days

I manifest boat trips wherever I go,
It's my happy place allowing me to flow...
The elements of the water & the air,
Has me free flowing wind in my hair...
It lights me up in so many ways,
Makes me so happy having mermaid days...

In My Heart Forever

It has hit me hard the realisation I had,
The emotions, the confusion was making me sad...
I've already seen the future of me & you,
But maybe you don't yet know what is true...
I've always said I want my freedom,
But what I really want is you in our nature kingdom...
Maybe it's trust I need to come back to,
And see how much this year I already grew...
Each time I go through another shift,
It's you there helping me lift...
Reminding me what matters in the now,
All the confusion fades away somehow...
But I still see the vision of us together,
It's been present in my heart forever...
Because you are me and I am you,
This connection we share is beyond what we knew...
We are together in another time & place,
When I close my eyes, I just see your face...
I know deep down you choose me,
And you're not choosing me so I'll finally see...
This lesson and belief needs to be let go,
Then all the magical blessings will flow...

In Full Flow

It's actually comical this journey of ours,
Perfectly aligned to unlock all of our powers...
I know this all plays out with such divinity,
And I'm grateful to have had you so much in my vicinity...
However, this week of space,
Has bought me so much grace...
I can now see so clearly,
That you love me dearly...
And when I think I'm being rejected,
I can now be unaffected...
Because you want me by your side,
It's just me that tries to hide...
I see all the love you give me,
All the many subtleties I clearly see...
You are my dream man,
Us coming together was always the plan...
Once I come back to how worthy I am,
I would have past the final exam...
Then we will merge in the physical,
Letting go of being critical...
We can let our guards down,
And spread healing to all those around...

Pieces Of The Puzzle

My gentled quieted heart,
Gives me flash backs to the start...
Our souls agreed to meet again,
We knew exactly where and when...
Pieces of the puzzle I did find,
Once I let go of my logical mind...
I was guided to you,
My heart always knew...
You felt our connection from the start,
All along you've helped heal my heart...
Sometimes I wonder if you know,
That our mission is to help each other grow...
Because once we do,
What feels so true...
Is the vibration that we emanate,
Will help end any world debate...
The love and light that ripples out,
Is what our human experience is about...
I sometimes wonder your thoughts about this,
Do you feel or perceive this delicious bliss...
I wonder if of twin flames you are a believer,
Or is it me who perceives the perceiver...

In Full Flow

Whatever it is I know what's clear,
That no matter what I love you dear...
I love you regardless of how you feel,
That's how I know this is the real deal...
Despite the fact you're with someone else,
Just mirroring me to love myself...
And when I do love me,
There is nothing else I see...
Than the beautiful reflection,
In the purest form of perfection...
Maybe you don't even know how I feel,
Maybe it's in the physical I need to reveal...
I feel to open up to you,
To share what on my heart is true...
Deep down you know communication is coming,
No longer will I allow my heart to keep running...
Because what I crave is to be fully met,
And lack of honesty is what I regret...
So I vulnerably open my heart to you,
And I share what deep down you already knew...
Are you ready to meet me here,
Or is there still more I need to clear...

Over & Over Again

From something that happened when I was ten,
Had me creating a block over and over again...
I lost the trust in relationships at twenty,
The pain that's caused has been plenty...
I'd choose the men that wouldn't choose me back,
Because I was coming from a place of lack...
Lack of self-worth & respect,
These inner words of hatred I would inject...
The belief was always so clear,
Any man I like will disappear...
So I put up a wall around my heart,
Then no relationship will ever start...
I would sabotage to stop any future pain,
Not realising I was making it remain...
I needed to respect & value myself,
So it will be mirrored by everyone else...
What if I opened my heart & was truthful,
I question, is this thought useful...

Support Yourself More

My passion and mission is to be of service,
But if I don't honour myself, it is a disservice...
Sometimes I need time out to go within,
That's when the downloads begin...
I'm seen where I am to go,
Things I could not possibly know...
If I was relying on my logical mind,
My intuitive gifts I would not find...
So the time I take to tune out,
For me is what it's all about...
Be supportive is what the whispers say,
It starts with self every single day...
So how can you support yourself more,
Before you even step out the door...
Breathwork, meditation & movement when I wake,
Then cold water & in the sunshine I will bake...
Topping myself up with vitamin D,
Then the sunshine flows out of me...

Ready To Open Again

I laughed at the cards I pulled out today,
And wondered what the words wanted to say...
So I put my pen in hand and start to write,
The message will soon be in my sight...
My intention has been to clear within,
I wanted to release the energy of him...
He was toxic and abusive in all forms,
Life with him was an abundance of storms...
But what was it in me that chose that pain,
I needed to heal within so it wouldn't remain...
So I made a commitment to myself,
And I blocked out everyone else...
If an amazing man came my way,
My body wouldn't trust what he would say...
I'd put a shield up when it comes to sex,
Because of the trauma I'd held from my ex...
I've spent much time healing from then,
And I'm now seeing what comes from this pen...
It's time to take the risk with that special man,
Your body is ready for him to help you open again...

Learning To Unlearn

What will it take to forgive them all,
Allowing any stories you've created to fall...
Knowing everyone is always doing the best they can,
Maybe not knowing when the pattern even began...
Because we are all learning to unlearn,
So much conditioning we need to burn...
We all learn at a different pace,
Let's all hold each other with such grace...
Knowing that each & every human being,
Deeply craves to be loved and truly seen...
Feeling a gentle acceptance between you & them,
Coming back to a pure state of oneness again...
Detachment from the ego is the key,
Living in the present moment to feel so free...

Face The Fear

I was keeping quiet and staying safe,
The thought of sharing my truth felt unsafe...
But I needed to face my fear,
Allowing this story to finally clear...
The pain of being rejected over & over again,
Never being fully met by men...
Was it actually me they would not choose,
Or was it my heart that would refuse...
The heart wall I'd put in place,
From when it began, I could not trace...
But I'm now done with choosing that,
Coming from any form of lack...
The time has come to accept & rechoose,
Knowing my best friend, I do not have to lose...
Because its unconditional love at the core,
Our relationship doesn't need to be any more...
We can be with nature on the land,
Together helping each other to expand...

The Ripple Effect

Do you know that feeling of encouragement,
It's that helpful support without judgement...
It may come out of the blue,
It may be foreign & new...
Maybe you've never experienced it before,
And now you're wanting to give it more...
Sometimes it may be a simple smile,
That helps someone walk that extra mile...
Or maybe you asked a stranger 'how's your day',
And you took time to listen to what they had to say...
That person sitting all alone might need to talk to someone,
And is almost giving up hope that day will ever come...
So please know we all crave that connection,
And if it's purely sent in the right direction...
The ripple effect from this simple act,
May steer them back on the right track...
So how can you include acts of kindness in your day,
Allowing your heart to lead the way...

{ 100 }

Releasing The Pain

Day by day one step at a time,
Knowing deep down everything is fine...
The message is now very clear,
And I know there is nothing to fear...
It was just some grief that needed to be felt,
From a past life, it had been dealt...
It wasn't his, it was always mine,
He was just the mirror to the divine...
Illuminating what I needed to see,
To release the pain I held inside of me...
I'd betrayed him in the past,
No longer did that guilt want to last...
Yet I'd made a promise I wouldn't do it again,
So I closed off my heart to any other men...
It was a karmic contract I'd put in place,
I now choose to remove that with ease & grace...
To create space for what wants to come through,
For what in this life feels so true...
No longer attached to any guilt & shame,
It's me I no longer need to blame...
Time to refocus the energy on me,
That amazing feeling of being so free...

In Full Flow

As I feel myself drop back into flow,
I feel the freedom of letting go...
The lightness washes through my being,
As I'm reminded it's safe to be seen...
I was guided here for a reason unknown,
I know it will make sense I will be shown...
It's coming back to that trust within,
Allowing this next chapter to begin...
It's brilliant how these lessons appear,
Presenting what is ready to clear...
I've got an amazing teacher in this guy,
And I'm grateful for all these tears I cry...
Because with every tear that I shed,
It allows me to be in my body instead of head...
Daily movement is the key,
Dancing and feeling so free...
Each day I do the things I love,
Allowing the messages from above...
Not allowing past pains to be a distraction,
From what is a true soul to soul attraction...

{ 101 }

Letting Go

She let go of the need to please another,
Seeing the patterns passed down from her mother...
She lets go of the wall around her heart,
So the new beginning could finally start...
She lets go of the emotions stored within,
To allow a new level of love to begin...
She cries out any tears,
Releasing any of the fears...
She drops anyone else's pain she is holding,
Allowing her to be in her feminine flowing...

Be Still

Be still, keep quiet, the message was clear,
And in that moment the tears started to appear...
All that hurt & pain inside,
Tucked in anywhere it could hide...
There were words that I needed to say,
It didn't matter the outcome at the end of the day...
I spoke what was on my heart,
That deep down it had been from the start...
In presence the fear melted away,
As I said what I needed to say...
But nothing changes between me & him,
I don't want it creating tension within...
So I must honour what feels right for me,
Taking alone time by the sea...
Each day I honour and appreciate self,
Not worrying of the needs of everyone else...
I feel that peace come back within,
As this next chapter starts to begin...

Larimar

The crystal that looks like the ocean,
Has me flowing and in motion...
I hadn't connected with it for so long,
Forgetting where I must belong...
It brings me back home,
To the inner light I roam...
Being of service is why I'm here,
Doesn't matter in what career...
Free flowing is what I miss,
It brings me my inner bliss...
Being of service doesn't mean carry others pain,
Holding it for them so it won't remain...
It means standing in light and love,
The frequency will be channeled from above...
People don't always see or feel the depths of what I do,
I am a channel for source consciousness to come through...

The Truths We Can't Hide

I cleanse myself of any outside energy,
Because I was feeling full on lethargy...
I initiated the chat to share my truth,
Illuminating the pains from my youth...
I surrendered knowing I couldn't be met back,
But I trusted that wouldn't throw everything off track...
But when we need to be cracked open wide,
It's these truths we simply can't hide...
I'm reminded to come back to trust,
Surrender to the process is a must...
If what I shared makes him run,
Then he is definitely not the one...
He again is just a mirror for me,
Illuminating what I don't want to see...
Because when it's him that runs away,
I now see the reflection that is at play...
Where is it I run from opening,
The one thing from him that I'm hoping...
But I'm not embodying what I desire,
So I'm presented with a fake mirror to admire...

Self-Sabotage

The lessons that have been on repeat,
The ones that make me want to retreat...
To stay in the shadows dimming my light,
But I'm being called to shine so bright...
There is a deep purpose in this,
Because it's my light that people miss...
Some may not see all that I do,
But deep down I know what is true...
I am here to birth movements into this reality,
Through the masculine & feminine duality...
But I must remember not to self-sabotage,
At times for me this proves to be hard...
I must always follow my passion each day,
And write to see what the words want to say...
I am the channel to the divine,
All that is for me, I will align...

Deep Healing Happening

I follow my inner knowing,
Listening to what the actions are showing...
The deep healing happening inside of me,
Is the final piece to have me feel truly free...
Lifetimes of carrying this pattern around,
Integration occurring now on this sacred land...
He has been my teacher, co-worker & soul mate,
But I got confused that meant he was who I was to date...
We share the perfect mirror for each other,
Which does not mean he is to be my lover...
He is who I'd always wished for in a best friend,
But there were patterns I needed to transcend...
This week as I've dropped into meditate,
I'm reminded to trust the magic of fate...

Is It True

Let go of the story playing in your mind,
In the present moment the truth you will find...
Ask yourself is this story true,
Or did it appear out of the blue...
Is it just emotion from the past,
So it can be felt to no longer last...
Maybe there is something you need to communicate,
That one thing that makes you procrastinate...
But when we speak the truth on our heart,
It illuminates when that story did start...
Allowing you to create energetic space within,
As a new depth of awareness starts to begin...

{ **108** }

Sister

Today is the birthdate of my sister,
Reminding me how much I miss her...
She has been there from my birth,
The day I chose to come down to Earth...
We grew up camping on the land,
And spending time on the beach in the sand...
There were moments when we didn't get along,
But I'm grateful for this family we belong...
We've travelled to many places,
Along with seeing many horse races...
Together we have had so much fun,
And those times are not yet done...
She may currently live in a different state,
And the border closures are making us wait...
But at the core there is only love,
That is always the message from above...
My family means the world to me,
And one day I know they will see...

Sailing Adventure

When I'm in my full flow,
I'm shown where I need to go...
Just like the wind in the sails,
We flow down the ocean trails...
So many islands to explore,
And diving to the ocean floor...
The gentle rock as I sleep,
The sea breeze feels so sweet...
Crystal clear water all around,
So much beauty to be found...

Island Dance

Dancing with the energy of the land,
My inner self can understand...
Activations coming through me,
Only beauty I can see...
Treasure everywhere I look,
On this island called Hook...
I looked up to see a mountain goat,
And then the silhouette of the boat...
A deserted island all to myself,
Enjoying the energy without anyone else...
Time in solitude is what I need,
It's my happy place that's agreed...
I top up by doing what I love,
Always listening to my guidance from above...
To be of service but me first,
In nature around water quenches my thirst...
I've learnt the hard way dehydrated of life,
That's how I know I'd make a terrible wife...
Because freedom is what I crave at my core,
When able to go where guided I need no more...

Triggers

They are the gateway to our healing,
The past conditioning gently peeling...
The feeling when the triggers arrive,
A feeling that you can't disguise...
It's there to be witnessed and felt,
For you this gift has been dealt...
It is a gift that you'll eventually see,
If you ask what is this teaching me...
What is the mirror reflecting back,
The exact thing that is keeping you off track...
Pay attention to the triggers that come your way,
See the patterning that is at play...
Take ownership of where it all started in you,
And see in the now moment what is true...
You can choose to heal that pain,
Or you can choose for the pattern to remain...
Sometimes it's best to process in our own space,
Sitting alone with the inner demons we must face...
But then comes the waves of peace,
As you allow those feelings or emotions to release...

Power Of The Mind

There is a heat I can't describe,
It's crippling to my vibe...
Days spent trying to keep cool,
Dreaming of an ice-cold pool...
Craving of some air-conned space,
Or just a cooler place...
The discomfort is making me stronger,
Instead of running when I can't take it no longer...
I feel the fire within,
And any agitation it may bring...
What is it trying to teach me,
It shows the parts of me that are not yet free...
The attachment to the heat,
But that is something I can beat...
The power of my mind,
Is a superpower of some kind...
I have the power to feel the cold,
My mind listens to what it's told...
I choose to feel the cool breeze,
Flowing through this day with ease...

Energetic Shifting

I'm going through a Transference Shift,
I'm reminded that this is such a gift...
I just have to surrender to it all,
Let spirit catch me as I fearlessly fall...
I've been sent to this place for a reason,
Maybe for a lifetime or maybe just a season...
But this much I know is true,
I'll look back one day seeing how much I grew...
All the triggers are a gateway to my healing,
The layers are just rapidly peeling...
Opening me up to what's yet to come,
I celebrate all the work I've done...
I'm craving to be held in a loving embrace,
By someone pure who moves with grace...
I'd love a base to call my home,
But with the freedom for me to roam...

My Desires

I'm calling in time on a boat,
It's above the water I like to float...
Serving people on beautiful islands,
Places where my soul deeply understands...
The sound of the ocean,
Creates my flowing motion...
I am calling in being valued for my support,
And I'm grateful for the lesson I've been taught...
I'm calling in my divine man,
One that is my biggest fan...
One that is willing to go to the depths,
One that loves me with no regrets...

{ 115 }

Paradise Bay

Sleeping on a secluded island,
My life is never ever bland...
I've created the life I dreamt of for so long,
Some areas of life might have felt wrong...
But that was my signal that change was in the air,
The moment things started to feel unfair...
If my life ever stops to flow,
I know there is somewhere new to go...
So I remind myself to just trust,
I know from past experiences it's a must...
Life had a special plan for me,
One that I could not yet see...
I felt the pain of this rebirth,
But I deeply trusted Mother Earth...
The greater the pain,
The bigger the gain...
So I knew good was on the way,
I was being sent to Paradise Bay...

New Approach

Find a new approach not allowing the old versions to repeat,
You're a Goddess & deserve a man that can see you're a real treat...
Reach a new level of understanding for yourself,
Know that you are more important than anyone else...
Get support from your guidance team,
They'll help you get the life you dream...

Telepathic Connection

He is so tuned in and knows me well,
Even with no contact he can really tell...
He knows when I'm talking about him,
He knows as soon as I begin...
He reached out to check on my heart,
Was that his game or has he also felt it from the start...
Just like me it's safer to run,
Before any relationship has begun...

The Discomfort

The sound of bitching in my ear,
Is something that's too much to hear...
I see everyone as love,
That's my guidance from above...
We are all healing at our own pace,
Someone being slower, does not make them a disgrace...
I really felt the discomfort in me,
I tried to change the topic so peacefully...
In future I must just walk away,
Not be around the bitching at play...
I'm in full control of where my energy goes,
I get to direct & decide where it flows...
Making sure it's for the highest good of all,
Always choosing love & knowing it's my call...

Pulling Away

I feel you feeling me pull away,
And this is not a game I'm trying to play...
But you wanted space from me,
And I guess you can finally see...
That I'm not like other women you know,
I will stay true to where I'm guided to go...
I knew I had to speak from my heart,
That I'd loved you from the start...
And regardless of how you feel,
My love for you is the real deal...
We hold puzzle pieces for each other,
We don't necessarily have to be each other's lover...
I'm just here to grow and evolve,
You're a mirror for everything I withhold...
Its confronting yet true,
And that is why I love you...
And I know I can help you grow too,
If you are ready to uncover what's true...
I'm here either way,
In many dimensions we play...

Drifting Away

I'm drifting away to this place I call home,
Through the rainforest I would like to roam...
Connected to this land beneath my feet,
Feeling the gratitude of being guided to this retreat...
Spirit had a plan for me all along,
Guiding me to where I do belong...
Surrounded by clear water & lots of trees,
I feel a cooler temperature with the breeze...
This island had been calling my name,
It was clear with what wasn't to remain...
The challenges I faced to help me grow,
Were leading me down a path I had to go...
Many fears I had to face,
As I was calling in a magical place...
And to create space for something new,
We are shown what is not true...
Those people, places or things will fade away,
Leaving a clear vision of truth at the end of the day...
Showing you how to be aligned again,
There will be old patterns you need to transcend...

Breakthrough The Pain

We all have choices to make,
At times there will be promises to break...
But if you come back to your heart,
Don't deny what you felt from the start...
I know it's easy to run from this love,
But that was not the plan from above...
We are here to break through the pain,
So our closed hearts don't have to remain...
But don't get swept up in the hype,
Because your followers they could just wipe...
So if you are just chasing the numbers,
Take note of the underlying messages...
Telling people you need a big following,
Instead of trusting your inner knowing...
If Instagram wasn't even a thing,
What would all these women bring...
Would you choose to be with them every day,
Or would you notice the pattern at play...
Because I can see it clearly from here,
And it repels me to not come near...

Window To The Soul

I looked into the eyes staring back at me,
Suddenly I was in awe at what I could see...
Everything was so clear,
Lifetimes all so near...
Neither of us wanted to look away,
As we were seeing what the eyes had to say...
Are we in a portal somehow,
Why is this all happening now...
Faces morphing before our eyes,
Any shadows we could not disguise...
Allowing ourselves to be truly seen,
Seeing all the lifetimes that have been...
Tears forming in my eyes,
My angels weren't telling me lies...
I knew something magic was coming my way,
I just trusted what they had to say...
Then he appeared in full sight,
His inner light shining so bright...

Uncover The Shadows

Where did my friend go,
We fell out of flow...
All because I shared what was on my heart,
What deep down had been from the start...
But I'm here to learn and grow,
And uncover the shadows I do not know...
I don't want to stay stuck,
Or be hit by another truck...
So I follow my inner guidance each day,
Leaning into the discomfort of what I'm to say...
Maybe there aren't many that can meet me in this place,
Until there is I'm happily single living in my own space...

{ 124 }

Eagle Vision

This day a year ago,
An eagle told me where to go...
So I trusted in that vision,
Even though my mind tried to cause a collision...
I went to order something to eat,
It was a mermaid bowl and ultra-sweet...
I sat down where I was guided to,
In a moment then appeared Ru...
But I didn't know this guy,
He smiled and wasn't at all shy...
He ordered food and sat down with me,
Chatting for hours speaking so effortlessly...
I felt and saw I'd be travelling with him,
But there were a few things needed for that to begin...
I needed to leave that other retreat,
It was an old pattern on repeat...
I also needed to purchase a van,
Even though I'd thought I'd do that with a man...
But life still likes me in full flow,
So I can be guided where I need to go...

Mirror Self

I see you probably more clearly than you know,
I see the game you play where everything is on show...
Needing validation from anyone else,
Escaping from truly being by yourself...
I know where you're at because I've been there before,
And I agree, why does anyone want this chore...
But what if you truly took this time,
To go within & connect to the divine...
You'll see there are many gifts for you,
And you'll see at your core what is true...
When you run from you, you run from me,
Because I'm the truest reflection you'll see...
So tell me, what makes you want to run,
Before you've even let the process begun...
I know your strength will find the way,
And you'll probably never want to hear what I say...
So I trust one day you'll eventually see,
That I love you because you're a reflection of me...
That is love in the purest form,
Holding the mirror as the other is reborn...

Path Of Healing

I committed long ago to this path of healing,
For some it may not sound very appealing...
But as the layers peel and I grow,
I find there is more I didn't know...
So I continue to dive to the depths,
Uncovering any shadows I had kept...
Kept hidden from my sight,
But now I see them so bright...
When I heal me, I heal you too,
It's a gift from me to you...
It's all in the energetics that I feel,
Then I know what I still need to heal...
Life rewards me along the way,
When I do the work, I also get to play...
Because this life gets to be enjoyed,
It was a condition when I was employed...
Employed to come here to Earth,
To help in this time of rebirth...
I just have to go where I'm guided to go,
Then through my hands the energy will flow...

{ 127 }

Truth At My Core

We are so connected like no space at all,
But this physical space helped me to fall...
To come back to the truth at my core,
We have done this many times before...
Each time I know it will pass,
The pain I feel will no longer last...
There are highs and lows on this ride,
But when you trust self, you don't need a guide...
What are you seeking outside of yourself,
The ego wanting validation from everyone else...
I will trigger you to awaken,
My presence will have you shaken...
And your choice is to run and hide,
Or take these triggers in your stride...
And heal what it brings up for you,
Ask yourself could this be true...

Hiding The Tears

Before I stepped out the door today,
I must have felt the energies at play...
The sun isn't fully shinning right now,
But I found my sunnies on somehow...
An old pattern of mine trying to hide,
Hiding the tears that I'd cried...
But this morning the tears hadn't yet come,
The process was starting before it had begun...
As I drove to my fave morning place,
A sign jumped out at my face...
It was about abuse towards women,
It bought up past memories from when...
A past relationship came to mind,
Abusive memories I'd tried to leave behind...
But they were still stored within me,
Illuminating more for me to see...
As I read a friends Facebook post it sunk in,
The depth of collective pain also carried within...
I know I'm not alone with what I've been through,
And I'm grateful for how much I grew...
But what I crave is to be safely held,
As these tears rapidly welled...

RACHEL HEANEY

To know that I am safe to feel,
My vulnerability is safe to reveal...
But is there a man that can hold me,
As his presence will set me free...

Ask The Question

Sometimes the hardest thing to do,
Is what life is asking of you...
Challenging you to face the fear,
Allowing any beliefs to disappear...
I want to expand and grow,
That is what I deeply know...
So I'm being guided to lean in and ask,
And it seems like the scariest task...
But I need to ask for what I need,
Knowing that I deserve to receive...
And if my need can't be met that is ok,
Because that was never the challenge at the end of the day...
The initiation came from me voicing my need,
The emotions that bought up have now been freed...
And if my need can't be met,
I haven't met my divine masculine yet...
But this is a massive piece of puzzle to my healing,
Layer after layer it kept revealing...
Asking for what I needed was what I had to do,
As I did, I felt my inner masculine say, I got you...

Gone Are The Days

Gone are the days where I shy away,
When I don't say what's on my heart to say...
Now that my self-sabotage is gone,
I watch as different connections transform...
Cleansing away where I didn't feel worthy,
Knowing now I am fully deserving...
I surrender and trust to a love so true,
One where I'm met and he wants this too...
All I have to do is speak from my heart,
And do this from the very start...
Don't assume they know how you feel,
If it's something you are yet to reveal...
Because what deep down you know,
If they love you, they will not go...
If what you yearn for is to be met,
Let go of the ones that can't or you will regret...
Spending so much energy waiting for them to see,
How powerful together you could be...
Walk away from those who can't meet you back,
Or you will continue living your life off track...

{ 131 }

Create Space

Surrender the judgements of anyone else,
Because all you need is to appreciate self...
Cleanse any projections thrown your way,
Don't take on board what they may say...
You can only take care of your inner reality,
Because that is the only key to feel the serenity...
Create space in your own energy field,
Solid inner foundations you will build...
If you are always in another's space,
It's your responsibility to find a secluded place...

Energy Doesn't Lie

Energy doesn't lie,
That, I cannot deny...
It's a gift to be able to feel,
The unspoken words so easily reveal...
If there is an untruth that is spoken,
My inner red flag detector is awoken...
Sensitive to people and their lies,
And I also can see it in their eyes...
Sometimes this gift can be a lot,
Knowing what is true and what is not...
And I don't even have to be in the space,
To feel what's going on in another place...
It's like I can read their mind,
Including anything that is unkind...
I choose to not engage with them,
As I don't want their energy disrupting my zen...
If you can relate to this too,
Know in your heart what is true...
Take space in your own energy field,
Solid energetic protection you will build...

Crossing Over

They say it comes in threes,
But I'd like it to stop please...
Because it's hurting the people I love,
As it takes their loved ones above...
I know it's all a matter of time,
Before we are called back to the divine...
I'm not attached to this human suit,
And I'm open if they need to recruit...
To bring about whatever lessons are needed,
I know everything has already been seeded...
So, no fear is needed at all,
Knowing we are all going to fall...
There is no predicting when that will be,
So you may as well continue to live free...

Heart Gate

My King, do you hear me calling,
Through this dimensional walling...
The time has come for us to unite,
Together our future is so bright...
Because we've healed the inner turmoil,
Allowing our hearts to uncurl...
It's safe to be held by each other,
And even be each other's lover...
Gone is the self-betrayal & hate,
We have now opened up our heart gate...
Allowing the love to ripple out,
That's what it was all about...
When we come together in love,
There are so many blessing from above...
Do you feel this connection now,
Give me a sign you're feeling it somehow...
Find a way to let me know,
You're ready for our love to grow...
To ripple out and create waves of change,
From our beautiful love exchange...

Committed To Grow

When we are both committed to grow,
We are shown what we didn't know...
Our connection is one the mind can't understand,
But I know the importance is starting to land...
When we come together as love,
Which is what we planned from above...
The ripple effect is beyond our greatest dream,
Travelling to all lands and in between...
There is no coincidence in our connection,
As there is a Christ Consciousness resurrection...
Together we are birthing a new frequency,
It's not something you've been able to see...
But I've felt it all along,
I knew my heart was not wrong...
It just needed to feel all that needed to be felt,
From all the past life karma it had been dealt...
I'm sorry for the pain I caused you in the past,
I'm so grateful that it doesn't need to last...
Because the layers have slowly peeled away,
And we're left with unconditional love at the end of the day...

Shadow Self

The shadow self may like to hide,
But the key is to look inside...
Get to know these parts of yourself,
Or you will continue to project onto everyone else...
Own those parts you don't want anyone to see,
Covered up by many distractions externally...
The need for so many material things outside of you,
Stops people from seeing deep down what is true...

Seeing The Patterning

Some parts of the self needed to die,
There will be many tears to cry...
But it's a must at the end of the day,
Seeing the patterning that was at play...
Seeing the mirror in front of me,
Showing me everything I didn't want to see...
Changing and shifting of my reality,
Now seeing things with clarity...
The path has now been cleared,
The dense energy has disappeared...
Don't be attached to what others say,
Just pay attention to the actions at play...
Can someone meet you where you're at,
If not, there is no point wasting energy on that...
My feelings around men have shifted,
So may upgrades I have been gifted...
I still love him dearly,
But I now see clearly...

{ 138 }

Mirrored Truth

Today is the anniversary of your birth,
Celebrating the day you entered this Earth...
Our souls agreed to meet,
From the first moment we did greet...
I recognised you in your eyes,
There was nothing to disguise...
I felt that love mirroring me back,
And I knew I was all good & on track...
The journey hasn't always been smooth sailing,
There were unconscious patterns that needed derailing...
So many moments of love and fun,
So many new chapters that begun...
You helped me open up my heart,
And were the inspiration for this poetic art...
Today you leave this beautiful beach,
Heading south sharing what you teach...
I know our connection is beyond what we know,
So I have full trust in letting you go...
If we are meant to meet in the physical again,
I'll just follow my intuition until I'm shown where and when...

Something Bigger Than Us

The sunshine came out again,
After I connected with my fave men...
The energy that we create together,
Is what will change humanity forever...
Our paths crossed for something bigger than us,
Staying together in love is a must...
The vibration is like no other,
And is supported by the Divine Mother...
When we all listen to the guidance within,
Sometimes those triggers will begin...
Illuminating what still needs to be healed,
All the shadows will be revealed...

She Shines The Light

She has so many gifts inside,
For too long she tried to hide...
Because not many understand what she does,
She channels energy and messages from above...
She is the bridge to the other realms,
For some her magic & gifts overwhelms...
And some have always seen her light,
As she silently helps others shine so bright...
She helps birth into this world so many things,
The energy and vibration that it brings...
Is to awaken the people that come into the space,
She brings an energetic transmission to any place...
Channeling light codes straight to their soul,
Helping them to let go of any control...
To activate their gifts hidden inside,
She shines the light so it's easy to find...
She may not tell you all of these things,
But you'll be activated by the energy she brings...
She's being doing this all for so long,
Helping others to awaken to their soul song...

All The Dedication

I see you,
I see a love so true...
I see all the dedication you've put in,
I also see a new chapter trying to begin...
What if there is a plan you can't yet see,
And of your current job you need to be free...
Know within yourself all the love you put into that job,
Know that the self-love you have they cannot rob...
Trust that leap into the unknown,
All the pathways will be shown...
You'll look back on this day,
Grateful for everything that got taken away...
You'll find a new sense of freedom within,
And that is when your life will truly begin...
This time of change is guiding the way,
Change is as good as a holiday they say...
So remember to enjoy all the simple things,
The love, peace & connection that life brings...
Knowing you are fully held & supported for choosing you,
New gifts & doors will open out of the blue...

Happiness & Love

Happiness is what we feel inside,
Then that pure joy is amplified...
Everyone who comes into our space,
Can feel the energy beaming from our face...
It is a powerful feeling,
It is so deeply healing...
But it all starts within,
When the heart starts to sing...
So are happiness and love the same thing,
Happiness is what unconditional love will bring...
So can you love yourself unconditionally,
Even the parts you don't want anyone to see...
Because when you feel that deep love for yourself,
It ripples out to everyone else...
So please sprinkle love wherever you go,
Because to love is to be happy, that is what I know...

Born As Pure Love

The light in our heart,
Has been there from the start...
We are born into this world as pure love,
We are all gifts of love sent from above...
We learn at a rapid pace,
From everyone that comes into our space...
We are sponges to the things we hear,
And sometimes we take on others fear...
We carry things that are passed down to us,
Until we realise letting go is a must...
We gently start peeling the layers back,
We start feeling ourselves coming back on track...
We let go of the pain,
So it will no longer remain...
We start feeling our heart,
And suddenly there is a spark...
The light is back to its old bright self,
Shining the love back to everyone else...

Love At First Sight

Sunrise you're such a blessing when you meet my eyes,
It's a love at first sight that I can't disguise...
You fill me up with sunshine,
The greatest gift from the divine...
A portal to a place many have been taught to fear,
Sunglasses stop the portal from being clear...
But eye gazing with you is such a treat,
Locked in from the second our eyes meet...
You hold so many secrets just waiting to be found,
I really miss you when you're not around...
You light up the path so I can see,
That you are a beautiful reflection of me...
I am a portal to the divine,
Within me all the dimensions I will find...
Easily roaming through this mysterious place,
I can teleport myself to another space...
Existing in many dimensions at the same time,
I just realised I am the divine...

Hidden From Sight

She had been kept hidden from sight,
Not wanting to upset anyone by shining too bright...
Every now and then she would be seen,
By those that knew where she had been...
They saw and felt her purity within,
They saw the way she helps others to win...
She loves to see others shine at the end of the day,
In the unseen realms is where she likes to play...
She births the new into this 3D reality,
And nurtures it with her love and purity...
If she is guided to cross paths with you,
She will see what in your heart is true...
And if your intention is to serve humanity,
She will help to make this a reality...
She'll feel if you fall off track,
And through the subtleties she'll call you back...
But if it's your heart you are not listening to,
You may lose this divine gift that was sent to you...

Cycle Complete

There is a cycle that is now complete,
It is not one that I will ever repeat...
I now fully see the power I bring,
To awaken someone's soul mission to begin...
There is so much value in what I do,
And the message is I need to value me too...
If there isn't an equal exchange taking place,
It's not the unworthiness I need to face...
I've now faced off with the darkness in every way,
And I now listen to the energy that is at play...
I walk away from anything that isn't flow,
Because the flow is where I'm guided to go...
I'm being called to another level of being,
Connecting to my angels, guides & support in the unseen...
I'm fully supported in every way,
Allowing more of my gifts to open each day...
Speaking my truth was what I had to do,
Illuminating what I see and feel is true...

{ 147 }

Love & Vitality

The thing that brings me joy is love,
It is when I notice the divine synchronicities from above...
The knowing without knowing how I know,
When I follow the guidance of where to go...
I feel gratitude for the sun, the sea & tranquility,
I feel the aliveness that nature brings to me...
I feel vitality looking at the crystal-clear ocean,
I feel the aliveness and freedom in my van Mocean...
I feel gratitude & joy for time on boats,
I see the love and vitality in a herd of goats...
The aliveness I feel when dolphins appear,
Knowing that I have nothing to fear...
I feel alive with love to feel fully met,
I feel joy for not doing things I would regret...
I feel vitality when a stranger smiles back,
Bringing my thought form back on track...
I love when the love I feel in me,
Becomes a loving reflection in my outer reality...

Natural Bliss

She greets us every day,
And spoils us in every way...
From the rising of the sun,
Knowing a new day has just begun...
Hearing the birds sing their song,
Reminding us that nothing is ever wrong...
When we feel our feet planted on the ground,
And we notice all the beauty that is around...
Any fear will melt away,
Because we are nature at the end of the day...
Constantly shown these reminders every time,
This is the key to help us truly shine...
So can you stop for a moment and just be,
In pure presence what do you now see...
This beauty has always been gifting to you,
You just needed to fully stop to admire the view...
Nature is a reflection of you and me,
Reflecting back our pure divinity...

Black Cockatoo Sign

Spirit bird I feel you all around,
I hear the cries in your beautiful sound...
I feel your support guiding me,
Always reminded that I am so free...
A celebration of the work I've done,
Reminding me to relax and also have fun...
I'm always exactly where I'm meant to be,
Therefore, I am always truly free...
When I trust in my higher self,
I won't get lost supporting everyone else...
I just need to do what lights me up each day,
And remember to always have fun and play...
I speak my truth even if I can't be met,
I live my life without regret...
Because regrets are a sign I don't trust myself,
Meaning that I've given my power to somebody else...
No longer will I give my energy away,
Unless there is an equal exchange at play...

{ 150 }

Feeling The Passion

There was a heat that made me run,
Before the fire had even begun...
But what is it I'm running from,
What is it that felt so wrong...
It was conditioning from the past,
But if I didn't want it to last...
I had to face that fear of the fire,
What if it was the key to all I desire...
But I ran to the water to escape the flame,
I didn't want to cause anyone pain...
Because I'd been burnt many times before,
So many that I'd stopped keeping score...
I wore a fire proof shield around my heart,
Not allowing any fire or passion to ever start...
Maybe I just need to call on my fireman friend,
To allow this past wounding to finally end...

Roller Coaster Ride

This journey known as life is like a roller coaster ride,
Sometimes we want to close our eyes and hide...
We've somehow committed so we need to trust,
This ride has started so the trust is a must...
So how can we best enjoy the trip,
Tune into your breath before the big dip...
Then surrender & let go of that fear holding you back,
Now you're in free flow and on the right track...
Embrace the joy and curiosity of your inner child,
Upside down, backwards & forwards this ride is wild...
Then after that there's the whip lash at the end,
You turn in shock to look at your friend...
Suddenly the smile appears on your face,
This chapter in life you now embrace...
Because roller coasters sometimes can be what we need,
They're the gateway to anything that needs to be freed...
At the theme park of life there are many choices,
To get on the ride we want we must use our voices...

Practice What You Preach

What does integrity mean to you,
Is it doing in your heart what feels true...
Maybe it's sticking to your morals each day,
Regardless of the distractions that are at play...
Listening to if your body says no,
Even if that means there's places you can't go...
Do you truly practice what you preach,
Are you embodying what you're trying to teach...
Because if people are looking up to you,
You have a responsibility to share what's true...
People have already been misguided by TV,
So please set a good example of what they need to see...
Stay true to the promises you make each day,
Be careful you're not manipulating the words you say...
Respect those that support along the way,
Don't get caught up with the ego at play...
If community is what you're about,
Make sure you're not leaving them all out...
The energy can be felt when your integrity is lacking,
And things in your business will start cracking...

Lone, But Never Alone

She was lone but never alone,
Because there were many places she would roam...
Seeing people that she would know,
Saying hello to friends wherever she'd go...
And in the times she was by herself,
She felt the energy of everything else...
The birds sang to her,
The dolphins swam with her...
The dogs cuddled her,
Nature held her...
She was fully supported in every way,
Her heart was filled with gratitude everyday...
Some might think she must be by herself,
But she has gifts not really understood by anyone else...
She can see what not many others can see,
This gift means that she is never lonely...

Mum

Today I celebrate my Mum,
She was there from the day my life begun...
She was holding me with a big smile on her face,
In that second, I knew I was in the right place...
I'd chosen well to end up here,
Surrounded by love and two sisters near...
Having three daughters must have been tough,
And I'm sure I didn't praise her enough...
But I'm really grateful that she is my Mum,
Not just my Mum, but a friend that likes to have fun...

What You Forgot You Knew

These changes we are going through,
Will illuminate what you forgot you knew...
You'll remember you agreed to come at this time,
The fact you're here is so divine...
So close your eyes and you will see,
You are a gift of love to help humanity...
So give free smiles wherever you go,
You may make someone's day, you never know...
Or maybe it's a hug that they need,
So any of their fear can be freed...
So they know that whatever choices they have made,
There is no reason to feel afraid...
Because we are all spreading love together,
And this ripple of love will last forever...
So embrace these changes of today,
Come back to what your heart has to say...
It's the fear that lives in the mind,
But in your heart it's love you will find...
So open your heart and let the love shine out,
Because this is what this life is truly about...

Whispers Of The Soul

She flows with the whispers of the breeze,
Guided through life with such ease...
It is one of her greatest gifts,
Through life she easily drifts...
Her life is like a dream,
So peaceful and serene...
This definitely wasn't always the case,
There were many shadows she had to face...
But she was committed to that journey within,
Knowing it was the only place she had to begin...
She knew the more work she did on herself,
Would be reflected back by everyone else...
Then all the beauty that she would see,
Was just a reflection of her inner reality...
She'd dreamed of an island home,
One where she was free to roam...
Surrounded by nature & bright blue sea,
A place where she was welcomed v-free...
Her gratitude is endless for this magical place,
She is constantly wearing a smile on her face...

Here For The Depths

Patterns and cycles come and go,
Some have them but will never know...
Because they've chosen a different path to walk,
It can make it difficult to have a deep talk...
I'm here for the depths & desire to be met,
I'll tell you all my shadows with no regret...
What you do with that is your choice,
We are all free to use our voice...
Some patterns had been playing out for so long,
And I'm not going to make anyone wrong...
Because everyone just plays a part for me,
Holding the mirror so I can see...
The things that have weighed me to the ground,
I no longer have to carry them around...

Flowing Love Story

Through all the highs and lows,
These are things she now knows...
She needs you in her sight,
You allow her to shine so bright...
The way you greet her with your wave,
Is something she has begun to crave...
The way you bow at her feet when you meet...
Is a greeting that no one else could beat...
The ripples of love you constantly send,
Your presence helping her heart to mend...
The love she feels for you,
Especially when you're feeling blue...
Is nothing like she has experienced before,
Every day she realises she loves you more...
She loves all the beauty you hold within,
You always manage to make her heart sing...
The times she doesn't feel her feet on the ground,
It makes her happy because she knows you're around...
You've swept her off her feet,
With this love so sweet...
Holding her with your embrace,
Allowing her to move with grace...

In Full Flow

And sometimes when you are near,
There are certain things she starts to fear...
But she knows she can dive to the depths with you,
Because you're there holding space for her to...
So she surrenders into the unknown,
Knowing so much beauty will be shown...
She thought this love she would never reach,
All those tears she would cry on the beach...
Then she realised her tears were a gift,
As she watched them as they would drift...
Down to the water creating an ocean of bliss,
She realised there was nothing she ever had to miss...
Because all the love in her heart,
Was being reflected back from the start...
The beautiful bright blue sea,
Reflecting back so she could see...
That her love spreads far and wide,
And is such a beautiful guide...
For those that need to learn to flow,
Surrendering to where they're guided to go...

Feeling Shy

Nervous but because of why,
What made me feel so shy...
Was I feeling shy for him,
Stopping anything before it would begin...
Who knows if I will see him again,
Did I just make him feel like a friend...
It's a habit I have to keep me safe,
Putting a shield around my heart just in case...
But if he is not the one for me,
I guess I'll be shown that so clearly...

Xmas Eve Grief

The grief washed over me,
My eyes flooded and I could not see...
All of a sudden it hit me hard,
I couldn't put on a brave façade...
What was it that wanted to be felt,
Is this collective grief that I'd been dealt...
Or was there generational healing taking place,
And that is why I'd been gifted this space...
Space all alone with no family around,
To allow these tears to fall to the ground...

Ending Of 2021

As we come to this ending of the year,
I look back and celebrate & cheer...
Everything that I have overcome,
All the times I felt, instead of going numb...
There were so many beautiful lessons along the way,
And I feel gratitude as I reflect back today...
I'm spending New Year's Eve on my island home,
Next year to the mainland I will roam...

New Year Revelations

The year I continue to follow my knowing,
I drop back into my feminine flowing...
I allow instead of chase,
Knowing my mission is not a race...
I wait for my King to initiate connection,
I allow his masculine to lead with direction...
So I can soften and open to him,
And allow our union to begin...
There is a gentle okayness in my being,
And it feels light and so very freeing...
Fancy that, that all I had to do,
Was listen to what in my body feels true...
To be in my flow is a gift to all,
As I allow any past patterns to finally fall...
I'll continue to serve the people with my love,
That was always why I was sent from above...

Just Free Flow

One step at a time, there is no rush,
She soaks up her surroundings so nature is a must...
The peace as the butterfly dances around,
All the music from the nature sound...
The trickle of water down through the rocks,
It just free flows without any blocks...
What a good teacher water is to us all,
Just surrender and trust the free fall...
Because like a whirlpool you surrender to let go,
Take in the view because you're in full flow...
Allow the water to nourish your soul,
Letting it wash away any control...
Just like the ocean the tides come & go,
In this human life there will be highs & low...
To stay afloat there are things you need to know,
Through the waves of emotions, you will need to row...

Nature & Hugs Instead Of...

Another year older, 20 years wiser,
She's always known the agender with Ph!z#r...
They want you to be addicted to their drugs,
But the best medicine is nature & hugs...
Ask, do they have your best interest at heart,
Have they cared about you from the start...
Say no to what they force onto you,
Giving you experimental drugs out of the blue...
What's in it for them is wealth,
Do they even care about your health...
And this v@x has had no use,
It's just a form of physical abuse...
Forcing a fluid into you against your will,
With no trials or proof that it won't kill...
Know that your body is your special home,
Not an open home for intruders to roam...

Choose Your Own Adventure

There is something to be birthed through me,
An interactive site or app is what I could see...
Sort of like a choose your own adventure,
Different paths the viewer will venture...
There will be poetry, sound healing, activations,
Card readings, energy clearings for all generations...
It's not just a one-time thing to explore,
Because each time you may open another door...
You'll find clues along the way,
Hidden messages in what the poems say...
Whatever in that moment you need,
Is what will find you to plant the seed...
And if there is more healing you desire,
The option is there for a DNA rewire...
Or if you require something else,
I'll recommend someone other than myself...

Natural Chemistry

Sometimes I feel the energy building,
For so long I'd forced up a shielding...
Blocking me from feeling the flow,
Of where the energy wanted to go...
But as I've cleared that block,
I've felt my sexual energy unlock...
I let go of any guilt feeling this way,
It is a natural chemistry at play...
I felt his presence from when we met,
He made my inner thighs get wet...
Breathing in and exhaling out,
This is what oneness is all about...
Two bodies blending as one,
Something special had just begun...
We entered a space of no time,
I must admit, it felt divine...
I didn't want it to end,
Together we so nicely blend...

Love Beaming

All is going well it seems,
Heart is open & the love beams...
It beams love for not just you and me,
But for everyone, even those I cannot see...
I am the channel to this higher Earth,
Yet it was something that I forgot during birth...
Now I know, I go for it with what comes through,
Because what you resist persists, I wish everyone knew...
But everyone awakens in their own timing,
In divine time, they will start shining...
But I must remember that judgement separates,
So I plant the seed and watch the ripple it makes...
Because each step can have a lasting impact,
But be gentle or the people might retract...

The Reason Why

The reason why I do what I do,
Is to activate others to help them shine too...
Because when everyone is awakened to their gifts,
I feel the consciousness of the planet as it lifts...
This is why I came down to Earth,
To energetically assist in this time of rebirth...
If I am guided to cross paths with you,
I'll remind you within what is true...
Always aligned with where I'm meant to be,
Working my magic in dimensions you may not see...
I'll be the portal to bring your mission to life,
In some way you could call me a cosmic midwife...
I'll allow you to go to the depths within,
To allow this new level of self to begin...

Stay Or Go

Should I stay or should I go,
Is it running or is it flow...
If I leave can someone take my place,
It is a role they can easily replace...
Is Port Douglas calling my name,
This island I am no longer to remain...
To connect back to my magic within,
And allow this next chapter to begin...
A place to birth my creations,
With no pressure or distractions...
Birthing the books that want to come through,
Creating a program and website too...
And a deck of cards want to be made,
From birthing my passions, I will be paid...

Signs Sent To Me

I pay attention to the signs sent to me,
Even the flicker, in the light I see...
Spirit, Angels, Soul, Light Beings, Source,
Always there guiding me on this course...
If I do what lights up my life,
That is when I'm a cosmic midwife...
And it gets to be as simple as that,
Even if it's just sitting on a yoga mat...
Because if that is where I can be,
That is what they truly want from me...
So I let go of any guilt I hold,
Or any of the stories I've been told...
I've done many years of pushing myself,
Trying to do everything for everyone else...
But that is not the reason why I came here,
I need to be, to keep my energy clear...
Because my frequency is like no other,
I am a channel to the star mother...
I am here to birth the new,
And maybe I'm here to help you...

Leap Of Faith

It's that time again,
I've been shown where and when...
The part of me that resists to leave,
Is the exact part of me I need to retrieve...
Rewriting the story from all those times before,
When the soul whispers I had tried to ignore...
So I continue to follow the guidance within,
And I'm open for this next chapter to begin...
I've been here many times before,
Always gifted with so much more...
I just have to take the leap into the unknown,
Because I know the next path is always shown...
That leap before I can fully see,
Yet I take that leap because I fully trust me...
I'm being guided to a place I'm yet to see,
Where the land has messages for me...
I don't listen to what the mind has to say,
I allow my feminine flow to guide the way...

Energy Clearing

I question why am I here,
Was there density I needed to clear...
Because when I stepped into that place,
The energy smacked me in the face...
I started energetically purging,
A rapid pace it was surging...
There was a tightness in my chest,
Now all I want to do is rest...
Allowing my body to transmute the pain,
So in this place it doesn't have to remain...
Maybe that's why I've been here all along,
Clearing the energy that doesn't belong...
And this week being my final time,
I just have to be the channel to the divine...
Spirit is sending me on my next mission,
Head up north was the message & vision...
So I trust where I am being shown,
And I'm proud at how much I've grown...

Time To Roam

It's my last night at my island home,
Spirit has a plan for me to roam...
And just like the ocean I love to flow,
My van Mocean takes me where I'm guided to go...
The Daintree has been calling my name,
The island retreat I'm to no longer remain...
As I reflect on everything that led me here,
I can't help but to stop and cheer...
And see how far I have come,
I celebrate this new chapter that has begun...
One where I see my value like never before,
And I know I'm worth so much more...
I'm open for opportunities coming my way,
I'm listening to what spirit has to say...
Waterfalls, nature & beautiful places to stay,
Connection, love and lots of fun and play...
This next chapter feels good in my being,
Continuing to live the life of my dream...

Guided So Clearly

Guided so clearly by the energy,
That's why they call me Ray Chi...
Because it is a gift I've had since birth,
And one of the reasons I came to Earth...
I'm a beacon of light,
I allow my light to shine bright...
Others can see the spark of love,
And it reflects all around & above...
Rippling out for all to see,
What they see is the channel in me...
Being the rainbow bridge from heaven to Earth,
Helping bring through what is to be birthed...
They feel an energy shift,
They feel their vibration lift...
That is one of my special powers within,
Allowing their next chapters to begin...
If they are drawn to the light in my heart,
It was always the plan from the start...
I openly allow the connection to flow,
Because deep down our souls already know...

Dream Lover

Can I lean on you when I'm not strong,
In your arms I know I belong...
I've been working on myself,
Not opening up to anyone else...
Because it's been you guiding me all along,
Illuminating if ever my alignment was wrong...
You guided me back on my mission,
Reminding me of my heart vision...
I feel you with me when I tune in,
Are you now ready for our union to begin...
I'm willing to lean into these edges with you,
For our growth there is nothing I wouldn't do...
Tell me are you ready to be of support to me,
My gifts in the world is what you want to see...
I just tell you what it is I need,
You help anything I create to succeed...
You light me up in the greatest ways,
Lots of fun & love for the rest of our days...
You love to photo, film & capture,
Which has my channel in full rapture...
We make the most amazing team,
Like some sort of magical dream...

In Full Flow

But this is not a dream, we are currently awake,
And you give so much love instead of just take...
You fully support all I do with a smile on your face,
From out of nowhere you appeared with such grace...
You greet me with a delicious hug,
In your embrace I feel so snug...
You are a warrior of light,
And the yummiest sight...
I finally feel that passion inside,
In your company I cannot hide...
You see me like no other man,
With you I know that I can...
Because anything is possible with love by my side,
And with you there I feel nothing but pride...
My lover, my best friend, my partner in crime,
When together, we both fully shine...
Now that you've come into my space,
I can't wipe the smile off my face...
This is the greatest love story of all,
I'm grateful for all the times I had to fall...
Because life was helping me release the pain,
So in me it no longer had to remain...
I had to journey back to my heart,
It was always the mission from the start...
For me to finally see the love in me,
Now it's a pure reflection of love I see...
Thank you for being my mirror to the divine,
In sacred union because we now align...
May we forever remember why we came,
So our pure love will always remain...

Wanderlust

I put pen to paper to see what wants to come through,
Maybe it's a message for me or maybe for you...
I feel a deep sense of wanderlust,
Exploring nature for me is a must...
Nature is my greatest teacher,
The trees, the leaves and every creature...
The trees stand strong in the ground,
From them, presence will be found...
To stand solid in the ground,
And observe everything around...
Gently flowing in the breeze,
They allow what is, with such ease...
They will hold you in their embrace,
Whispering wisdom into the space...

Cosmic Midwife

It's this time of year where I love to support,
Well according to memories on my Facebook report...
Two years ago, getting ready for Wildfire,
Running retreats has always been my desire...
We flew to Bali to run the Woman's Retreat,
Women ready for the deep work we would greet...
Holding space for what wanted to come through,
Witnessing how much all these women grew...
Spirit guides me to work in these spaces lots,
And it took me a while to connect the dots...
I'm here as a pillar of light to the divine,
Helping to activate your light to shine...
One year ago, another new team did form,
And in that energy C2BC was born...
There may be two main faces to the name,
But my energy and essence will always remain...
Because I help energetically birth into this Earth,
Missions that will assist with humanity's rebirth...

New Level Of Commitment

This last week has been a full activation,
And the most magical illumination...
I stepped into a new level of love for self,
And it has been reflected back by someone else...
I'd committed to myself like never before,
I ignored that voice telling me it was a chore...
I trusted my masculine within,
So this new level of commitment could begin...
I've been dating myself for a few years now,
Maybe I am my greatest love somehow...
Then I realised how real & true it feels,
And allowed my heart to open as it reveals...
That sacred union was within me,
Then my mirror appeared for me to see...
Is he the divine masculine I'd longed to meet,
Smiling at me and grounded in his bare feet...
His eyes a portal to the divine,
Illuminating the reflection in mine...

Cape Tribulation Illumination

Today I felt guided to come to Cape Tribulation,
Not knowing it was the place of illumination...
Everything becomes so clear to see,
That sacred union begins within me...
When I commit to myself,
It is reflected back by everyone else...
The energy in this place,
Illuminates what you're yet to face...
There are signs of fear at every turn,
But what is it that you came here to learn...
Is it love over fear,
Allowing fear to disappear...
Or is it to stay stuck in the hell you've created,
Is it for this love that you have waited...
Keep opening your heart keeping the fears away,
Trusting in love, not listening to what your mind might say...

{ 180 }

Memories & Lessons

Memories and moments from a year ago,
Not knowing how much I still had to grow...
My heart was still not fully open,
Holding up a shield from the many times it'd been broken...
Matters of the heart had always been hard for me,
There were things I didn't want to face or to see...
I grew used to being alone,
On my adventures I would roam...
Getting to know myself over again,
Letting go of any of the past pain...
Meeting myself like never before,
Realising there was so much to adore...
My self-love grew and grew,
It was the deepest love I knew...
I was committed to myself,
Then I was met by someone else...
They had also gone to the depths within,
And in that moment sacred union did begin...

Self-Love Journey

This message gets even more clear,
With every single passing year...
The love you seek from someone else,
First has to be met within yourself...
The illumination of memories from long ago,
I had no idea how much I had to grow...
My heart was not fully open,
From all the times it had been broken...
Matters of the heart held so many lessons for me,
Ones that took me so long to see...
I grew used to being alone,
On my solo missions I would roam...
Getting to know myself from deep within,
Allowing the journey deep into my heart to begin...
Facing all my shadows like never before,
Seeing that there is so much to adore...
My self-love grew and grew,
It was the deepest love I knew...
I was committed to myself,
And that love gets reflected by everyone else...
Every moment a new teacher will appear,
Illuminating anything within that needs to clear...

RACHEL HEANEY

So when you look in the mirror may you be kind,
Not allowing past pains or stories to come into your mind...
Just gently coming back into your heart,
Knowing you've been pure love from the start...
Now when you look in the mirror what do you see,
You'll see your divine love reflected back to beautifully...

Between The Lines

The soul whispers are getting louder now,
So I'm researching the details of how...
So I can create a poetry book for you,
To help you meet yourself in a love so true...
May the words that channel through,
Spark an activation within you...
Reminding you why you came to Earth,
And how best to assist in this time of rebirth...
Maybe all you have to do,
Is to learn how to love you...
Allowing that frequency to ripple out,
Maybe that is what your mission is about...
Just one step at a time in the direction of your heart,
Maybe that's when you'll create the greatest art...
Letting go of pressure of what you think you have to do,
Because your greatest gift is when you truly be you...
So when you read the words in this book,
Or you see the photos that I took...
Know that there is an energetic transmission taking place,
And I'm energetically holding you with such ease and grace...
If there is something that inspires you too,
I invite you to put pen to paper & see what comes through...

RACHEL HEANEY

Writing poetry illuminated so much for me,
Messages in the words for me to see...
It was creating a safe space of healing,
I never knew all these poems I would be revealing...
But because they helped me so much to grow,
They allowed me to drop into full flow...
If you are now reading this,
Take a breath, tune in and feel the bliss...
This book is fully infused with love,
It's one of my gifts sent from above...
So feel the energy that is coming through,
It's a soul-to-soul gift from me to you...

Commit To Yourself

How much can you commit to yourself,
And not be swayed by everyone else...
Those little things you tell yourself you'll do,
Do you commit to self and follow through...
Or do you let yourself down,
Losing your King or Queen crown...
I used to do this all the time,
Not knowing the loss was always mine...
Because if I can't even trust myself,
That trust won't be met by anyone else...
And if what you want is to be truly met by another,
Make sure to treat yourself as you expect from a lover...
Everyone reflects the mirror back to us,
So that self-trust is a must...

Outlet To Heal

The freedom to pick up a pen and write,
The words just appear in my sight...
No idea what wants to be expressed,
I write so those words won't be suppressed...
It is one of my fave outlets to heal,
Unconscious thoughts it may reveal...
Or maybe it's a message just for me,
One in the 3D reality I can't yet see...
So I trust when I am guided to write,
The divine guidance can be so bright...
So I allow the pen to just flow,
Then I'm presented with what I need to know...
I'm so grateful for this incredible gift,
And the way it helps me uplift...
Not just me but maybe you too,
Because sometimes it's a message for you...

Safe Space To Heal

The importance of being in a safe space to heal,
That safety allows the subconscious to reveal...
We can create this space for ourselves,
Or it can be provided by somebody else...
There has been this man show up for me,
He held that space so I could see...
All the things that were holding me back,
All the ways in which I was coming from lack...
He didn't run when my tears started to fall,
There was no judgement & he didn't put up a wall...
His presence allowed me to surrender deeper & deeper,
My nervous system thought, wow, he is a keeper...
But maybe he is just for this moment in time,
So together we could connect to the divine...
Our connection has been like no other,
And he is the greatest divine lover...
Allowing my body to open with his present touch,
This divine masculine is helping me heal so much...

Blessing In Disguise

This portal hasn't all been smooth sailing,
Some days it's had me waling...
Crying tears from long ago,
Showing me what I didn't know...
A blessing in disguise you may say,
I surrendered and said come what may...
Mirrors showing up wherever I look,
Giving me inspiration for this poetry book...
The portal to the heart to truly feel,
Allowing a new sense of self to appeal...
Seeing where relationships make me want to run,
If there is a challenge and it's no longer fun...
But I've stopped myself from running this time,
I sit in the discomfort & connect to the divine...
I feel what needs to be felt right now,
Then the discomfort fades away somehow...

Feeling It All

Any sort of control needs to be gone,
Before our sacred union can be born...
A connection that neither of us can deny,
If we said there wasn't anything it would be a lie...
We shared all our past hurts and pains,
And we picked each other's brains...
We had both also been the inflictor of the pain,
We didn't want that part of us to remain...
Yet we'd closed our hearts long ago,
Until cupid pulled out the bow & arrow...
This one day I was guided where to go,
I just had to trust and go as I know...
So I followed that guidance within,
That is when I was guided to him...
He said hi and asked about my van,
At this stage I'd given up on meeting a man...
We just chatted briefly about where we'd been,
We walked the same path but he I had never seen...
He then said goodbye and walked to his van,
I thought how nice, this man has a new fan...
And then as he drove past,
He opened his window and asked...

RACHEL HEANEY

Can I get your number from you,
In that moment his sexiness grew...
Because I desire a man to take the lead,
And I don't ever want to have to plead...
He messaged to say it was nice to meet me,
Brownie points for his masculinity...
The next day when we hung out,
I wasn't sure what our connection was about...
He commented on the crystal around my neck,
Then came in for a kiss and I thought what the heck...
There is a big gap in our human years,
But I'm reminded to let go of any fears...
It was the most amazing kiss,
My whole body was filled with bliss...
And he was very turned on it was clear to see,
I could feel him pressing up against me...
We wouldn't contain our connection,
It was a full-on public display of affection...
So long since I'd felt a strong connection with a man,
And I'd never even christened my van...
I was so sensitive to his touch,
I wanted to scream with pleasure so much...
A couple of days later we were still feeling it all,
For him my full body wanted to fall...
I'd set myself a celibacy challenge of a year,
It was the anniversary & I started to fear...
I allowed past trauma to take over my mind,
The surrendered bliss I again needed to find...
I went completely closed off to this man,
A second before I was his biggest fan...
Yet he held that space for my tears,
He listened as I shared my fears...

In Full Flow

I didn't feel any judgement from him,
I felt his compassion from within...
I didn't feel I'd hear from him again,
But I did and so many fears did transcend...

In A Haze

The last few days for me I've felt in a haze,
It's like I'm here but not here kind of phase...
I'm in the void during this portal of 22222,
An emptiness, a stillness and nothing else feels true...
I've questioned what is the point of this life,
Even had a stalker hang around me with a knife...
I no longer wanted him in my space,
So I got in my van and I left that place...
The light codes bring the darkness too,
Illuminating where you haven't yet grew...
I don't try to find peace in my mind,
As sometimes it's thoughts can be so unkind...
I ask myself what in this moment do I need,
To be held by the masculine as my emotions are freed...
Yes, I can hold space for myself,
Yet sometimes I crave it from somebody else...
I call on my King to reach out to me,
If you're committed to this union then let me see...
Send me a sign that I will know,
Allowing me to drop into my Ray-Chi flow...

Intimidated By Her Shine

She was a glimpse you had to the divine,
Yet you were intimidated by her shine...
She shone her light on the parts you didn't want to see,
She was there to help you set those shadows free...
You had the choice if you were ready to evolve,
Yet you allowed your fears to be involved...
And instead of the King you could have become,
You allowed the little boy within to run...
Now you've lost this rare gift that came your way,
Because you couldn't see the divine gift at play...
There are now so many beautiful lessons for you,
So you can live a life so pure and true...
She is now the one that got away,
Because you didn't listen to what your heart had to say...
In every moment there are many paths we can take,
And whichever you take is not a mistake...
Because we are here to evolve & grow,
There is one thing you need to know...
That we are truly never ever wrong,
As the path we walk is where we belong...

Full Circle Unravelling

Full circle to where my unravelling begun,
Remembering all the times I wanted to run...
Yet I faced all those shadows that appeared,
And I dove deep within as they disappeared...
Everything became so clear,
I didn't want anyone near...
Because this journey was one for the self,
I pulled my energy back from everyone else...
Some of these days were so hard for me,
And I really missed having community...
Yet life had created the perfect place,
Illuminating what I had to face...
A pilgrimage through my soul,
Letting go of any control...
The greatest gift of it all,
Was seeing I've got me when I fall...

I Couldn't Ignore Her

Last night I found myself watching a movie,
It has been many years since I gave up TV...
There was something I hadn't yet felt,
And this movie had me melt...
Melt away any shields around my heart,
I've been releasing this shield from the start...
My body went into trauma,
And I couldn't ignore her...
She shook uncontrollably as she cried,
Allowing the chains to untie...
Knowing there was some deep healing taking place,
She was so grateful for this movie that made her face...
Face all the times she runs away,
Maybe what she needs to do is stay...

I Didn't Want To See

Today has been one of those days,
Where I've felt in a deep haze...
As the waves rolled in on me,
It was through my eyes that I didn't want to see...
Because when I opened them, I was in shock,
From my visions I wanted them blocked...
The energy was dragging me under,
I couldn't take it no longer...
So I allowed the feelings to be felt,
Even if it wasn't to me, they were dealt...
Ships all lined up in the ocean,
Just a glance bought up so much emotion...
They were robbing our sacred land,
But do they even know or understand...

Energy In Motion

The water holds a certain frequency,
Sometimes what the eyes can't see...
But I've always felt the waves of the ocean,
As it hits me with every single emotion...

Grounding Back In

Grounded back into this sacred land,
A feeling many wouldn't understand...
This headland holds energy for me,
It tops me up and does it for free...
It's my fave way to start my day,
Bare feet on the sand I like to play...
Listening to the waves roll in,
As the sunrise starts to begin...
I get my elixir to start my ritual,
This is something that is habitual...
Then I head up the hill,
I see the sunrays gently spill...
Down through the trees onto the track,
Aww...It feels so good to be back...
The coolness of the leaves,
As they're met by a slight breeze...
The energy feels good in here,
I'm so glad I now have this so near...

{ 195 }

Meditated Bliss

Trusting the divine nature of all,
Yesterday I started to fall...
A merkaba of meditated bliss,
Oh, that feeling I had missed...
Everything started spinning,
A new vibration was beginning...
I surrendered and let go,
The activation continued to flow...
Today when I woke, life had a plan,
Forced to drive a little in my van...
I aligned with a fellow light being,
A beautiful reflection I was seeing...

Powerful Equinox

This day is a powerful one,
From my shadows I cannot run...
Because to run would be cheating myself,
And that ripples out to everyone else...
Life is asking me to settle and ground,
Because in that stillness my gifts are found...
To fully commit to me,
Allows me to feel so free...
To stick to a routine each day,
Also listen to what the whispers say...
I was confused about where I was to land,
And my mind was busy trying to understand...
But when I came back to trust,
I was reminded the trust is a must...
When I surrendered coming back out of my mind,
The place I was calling in I finally could find...
I was feeling the valley surrounded by trees,
Even though I'd really miss the sea breeze...
A beautiful space to myself I had found,
And possibly even a massage space including sound...

Falling Into Place

Things are coming together & falling into place,
I'd been calling in my own home space...
Surrounded by nature in the valley is what I felt,
And of course, that is what the universe has dealt...
My own studio apartment to call my home,
Barefoot on the land I will be able to roam...
The stability right now is what I need,
So my feminine is safe to be freed...
To create, to heal, to flow & to know,
That she is always guided where to go...
She'll start her day committed to self,
So she can then spread the energy to everyone else...
Making her way down to the village café,
Meeting amazing new souls every single day...
Finding her tribe and beautiful connection,
As many new paths show a new direction...
She'd been craving this for so long,
A stable base where she does belong...

Dad

This is a little poem about my Dad,
For being his daughter, I am so glad...
The many ways he had helped me grow,
Like a library he retains so much info...
He took us all camping as we grew up,
Showing us how connection to nature fills our cup...
Being in nature getting to explore,
Always showing us there is so much more...
Getting to climb Uluru when I was three,
I was taught what it's like to feel so free...
I'm so grateful for all his support along the way,
And how he brings laughter with the things he may say...
He even helped me set up my van home,
So this beautiful country I could continue to roam...
Dad, I don't think I ever praised you enough,
But I thank you for all your hard work and love...

She Will Shine Again

The weight of the world with every step,
Is she still clearing karmic debt...
Stories created in her mind,
Ones that are not at all kind...
She knows that when she feels this way,
Soon something magical will come her way...
She allows herself to feel the pain,
So no longer it will remain...
She longs to be back in her true flow,
She wants to feel a clear yes or clear no...
Part of her wants to hide herself away,
But is that just her pattern that is at play...
Or is life asking of her to honour herself,
Before she can be around anyone else...
And when she trusts in the feeling,
It's what helps with the healing...
Finally breaking this cycle for good,
So deeply engrained she never thought she could...
But she can and she will shine again,
Only divine timing will know when...

{ 200 }

Angus

Angus, my angel, my guide, my love,
Always guiding me from above...
Yet I'd forgotten that he is always there,
But he came through to guide me where...
To where I need to anchor into the land,
It will teach me what I need to understand...
Reminding me of Angus's mission,
Showing me his New Earth vision...
Knowing that it's not specific people I'm meant to see,
It's the land that has messages for me...
It's going to hold me and be my home,
So from that base I can roam...
Knowing I've always got a place to rest,
That is when I do my soul work best...
I'm going to make it welcoming & energetically clear,
All the sacred messages from the land I will hear...
Candles, incense, oils and greenery,
It will be the most beautiful scenery...

Cleansing Rain

The cleansing rain comes down some more,
A drop for every tear but who's keeping score...
The rain a symbol of the tears we all hold back,
But it's what we need to allow, to keep us on track...
Or that track will be swept away,
And we will feel lost at the end of the day...
So let this rain be a reminder to always feel,
Because like Mumma Earth we also need to heal...
These tears are a beautiful gift,
So try not allow your mind to drift...
To drift away to a dark place,
Where all the fear you will have to face...
Stay grounded as best you can,
Knowing that soon the sun will shine again...
Like we sit in circle holding space for each other,
We also need to do that for our mother...
Mother Earth holds us through it all,
And she also needs to let those tears fall...
So each day lets send her love,
Behind the clouds the sun is shining above...

Village Life

I've found a beautiful place to land,
My bare feet in the grass they stand...
Listening to the birds rise with the sun,
I feel grateful this new chapter has begun...
Sunshine through the windowpane,
The sun came out after all the rain...
Welcoming me into my new space,
Nature also gets to thrive in this place...
Kangaroos greet me down the street,
Around every corner a new smile to greet...
Gratitude fills every part of me,
Everywhere I look more beauty to see...
Guided to the café to see some amazing peeps,
Now my neighbours surrounded by creeks...
Today I head to the valley to see a new retreat,
Where there are people, I am yet to meet...
To do my healing for the people who need it most,
I've done eight years working as a retreat host...
It's a role that completely fills my heart,
Supporting people as their awakening does start...

New Home Space

A new place that I can call my home,
From there I'll be able to roam...
Down to the café as I soak up the land,
It feels so good most wouldn't understand...
Then I drive down to the retreat,
The energy out there could not be beat...
Feeling my creativity coming back more each day,
As I listen to what the whispers gently say...
Birthing something new into this Earth,
To assist humanity in this time of rebirth...
What will light me up and serve them too,
When I follow my intuition and what feels true...

The Little Subtleties

Every little subtlety can be felt,
And plays a part in what you're dealt...
So make sure you stay true to you,
To live a life that supports you too...
If your body is telling you 'no',
Listen to it to drop into full flow...
Any 'no' that you try to ignore,
Will add up as the body will keep score...
The mind may try to trick you,
But feel in your body what is true...
Otherwise, you will fall off track,
And energy you will start to lack...
When you honour your 'yes' and your 'no',
You will be in alignment wherever you go...
The greatest feeling for me is full flow,
It's why I listen to what my body wants me to know...

Star Sister

Today I get my star sister to receive from me,
I'll be the channel for all that she needs to see...
Let the activations channel through,
Reminding her of everything she ever knew...
May I hold the space so beautifully,
To gift to my star sister so divinely...
I can't even plan the treatment in my mind,
Because I'm just the channel of some kind...
Cards, crystals, oils and sound,
Sending her to the cosmos and then back to ground...
An activation for each other is the exchange,
This is what spirit has arranged...
We don't even know but we really do,
This life being such a gift for her & me too...
We will be both topped up and upgraded,
This journey is going to be so sacred...

Integration Angel

The integration is real,
See what it has to reveal...
Yesterday an activation took place,
Clearing the fears that I needed to face...
To allow everything to channel through,
Reminding me of everything I knew...
The beautiful angel that came to me,
She is the purest light I could ever see...
She is an inspiration to humankind,
Allowing them to let go of their ego mind...
She is such a gift and so divine,
I'm so grateful to have shared this moment in time...

{ 207 }

Blissful Activation

Last night something came over me,
A channeling that had me feel so free...
Energy pulsing through my entire being,
More than I've ever felt or seen...
My body was being upgraded,
And oh my, it felt so sacred...
My hands were moving at a rapid pace,
Synchronised and moving with such grace...
Moving up my body and out to the sky,
My mind could not try to understand why...
I was surrendered in bliss and awe,
And it kept going there was so much more...
Light language I've never heard before,
All my gifts and body I started to adore...
The kundalini energy running up my spine,
And it felt so magical and so divine...
Thank you for the magical activation,
I'll allow for all the integration...

My First Niece

I want to write a poem about a special someone,
I'll start from the beginning when it all begun...
I'd found out a magical gift was coming my way,
And wow, it sure did brighten up my day...
It was a little ray of sunshine,
A baby girl who was so divine...
I had just become an Aunty to my first niece,
And she was so beautiful & the picture of peace...
She flew to Hawaii before the age of one,
So much laughter from all her napkin fun...
Cheeky and cute with a smile on her face,
She would always bring love to everyone in the space...
Such a special gifted soul she has always been,
She'd pass on messages from Grandma Mary in the unseen...
But she wasn't unseen because Harper saw her face,
And would pass on messages with such ease & grace...
She is so smart always winning awards at school,
And she has her own style which is ultra-cool...
I'm so grateful for the time we have together,
I will love her so much forever and ever...

{ 209 }

Indigo Children

Their eyes light up with a sparkle of blue,
I know these Indigo Children know what's true...
They can hold an eye gaze like no other,
United with another star sister or brother...
Curiosity and aliveness in every step,
It's the presence when they feel met...
Can you see these gifted souls too,
Maybe one of them is you...

Finally Free Of The Story

I knew it was going to come to light,
I'd seen it in a past vision in clear sight...
Did I create it with my belief,
Just so I could feel more of this grief...
From not being chosen by someone I love,
One of my lessons I chose from above...
But I see it clearly now,
And I let go somehow...
It doesn't mean anything about my worth,
It's just a trauma I've carried since birth...
And I've allowed that story to continue to live,
So much attention to it I would give...
No longer will I carry that story around,
It's been weighing me down into the ground...
But first I make sure there's nothing left to feel,
And I ask myself is this story real...
Then I realise there is no charge left in me,
And I feel what it's like to finally feel free...
Free of a story that had consumed my mind,
Now that story I can no longer find...

{ 211 }

Embody Your Light

There is something wanting to birth through,
It's a soul-to-soul healing from me to you...
So you can embody more of your light,
And see all the beauty in every sight...
Oils, cards, crystals & breath,
To clear away any past fear of death...
Because you are here to help humanity heal,
As you breathe, the next step will reveal...
You'll be shown what you are to do,
And nothing else will feel more true...
Anointed with my channeled oil blend,
All your past life gifts you will befriend...
So place your hand on your heart,
This beautiful journey is about to start...

Receive, Feel & Heal

I find it odd that people don't allow themselves to receive,
Is it deep down that they don't really believe...
They don't believe they are worthy for a gift,
If someone offers, they quickly drift...
Away from the offering that was meant for them,
And then their same cycle loops again...
They say they are open to receive, feel & heal,
But it is their true belief, that they reveal...
I have been here many times before,
I've also walked through the receiving door...
When we truly are open to receive,
There are miracles for us to retrieve...
This can be a challenging task for some,
I invite you to open your heart instead of run...
Because when you receive you also give a gift,
And that gift will help humanity uplift...

The Art Of Relating

She had been called to a valley she knew,
She listened to that guidance that came through...
She found a place surrounded by nature,
And the relief she felt was so major...
She had to let go of so many things,
Knowing the gift that deep listening brings...
She allowed those things to fall away,
She went deeper within every single day...
She remembered what she had forgot she knew,
Each day her gifts and wisdom grew & grew...
She stayed cocooned & hidden from sight,
There was still something saying don't shine too bright...
Those whispers had been with her from lifetimes ago,
She knew that story was ready to go...
But there were some fears that were still existing,
So she started leaning into the areas she was resisting...
She started ten weeks of A.R.T. Training,
To illuminate the blocks still remaining...
Each week she would enter the unknown,
With no idea what shadows would be shown...
Then one week something profound took place,
All the love & support was hard for her to embrace...

RACHEL HEANEY

She is usually the one always holding that space,
The reverse for her hadn't always felt safe...
Previously she'd been shown if her emotions were to flow,
That she would be abandoned with nowhere to go...
There was trauma still in her being,
To the hot seat she was sent to be seen...
To receive the way people perceive her,
The positive & negative ways they receive her...
Sometimes it's our own shadows that we can't see,
And with the support of another, they can be set free...
In this case she was hiding to not be seen,
This was definitely an edge she needed to lean...
Her body went into a trauma release,
As she shook and cried out every piece...
Stories that taught her it wasn't safe to be seen in her tears,
Rewritten as she was held in love replacing those fears...
A room full of men and women loving on She,
She wasn't abandoned, she was held so lovingly...

Womb Healing

Her womb was calling for this healing,
She knew past pains would be revealing...
From all the times her boundaries won't met,
And all the encounters she has wanted to forget...
But the numbness in her womb wasn't to remain,
She was ready to release any of that shame...
She felt it may be so overwhelming,
But into the womb she was delving...
Her portal of creation,
A gateway to the star nation...
She chooses to allow herself to feel,
Ready for what her womb has to reveal...
Afterwards, she'll feel a deep state of peace,
As her gifts & creativity will increase...
Preparing her womb to birth something new,
An online portal to help others too...

The Greatest Gift

The journey is to always love what is now,
Allow fear & criticism to fade away somehow...
Always having a choice what we choose,
What do we feel when we watch the news...
Does it put us in an easeful state,
Or are we left with fear to navigate...
The first step to my healing,
Was to trust myself in the revealing...
Within my beautiful being,
There were answers to be seen...
Not always seen with the eyes,
Sometimes they like to disguise...
It was tuning into the subtle feeling,
And everything it was revealing...
My intuition became my greatest gift,
When trusting it my vibration would uplift...
This is why I'm so passionate to help you to tune in,
Allowing a life of flow to fully begin...

Up Until Now

Up until now it had seemed overwhelming,
So to everyone else's business I'd be delving...
But the time has come to share what's true,
I activate others to help them shine too...
My unique codes are here to help humanity,
Help them to come back to unity...
That unity first comes from within,
So that is where the journey will begin...
Instead of being so giving to everyone else,
We will bring that love & support back to the self...
Using the things that have most helped me,
Allowing our hearts to be set free...
Because when we can love our own being,
We can also connect to the unseen...
Allowing our intuition to guide the way,
Knowing we are divine source at the end of the day...

Time Just For You

Sometimes the hardest thing to do is decide,
Allowing everything else to fall aside...
To dedicate that time just for you,
To feel the alignment in what is true...
Letting go of seeking outside of yourself,
Letting go of supporting everyone else...
And bringing your energy back to your heart,
Loving the divine gift you've been from the start...
Through the resistance you love what is,
Time for you is the greatest gift...
You welcome this new beginning with ease and grace,
As you feel divine energy embrace the space...
Creativity overflowing your entire being,
Birthing things from the unseen...
Allowing you unique gifts to merge as one,
Your own activation portal has just begun...

Surrendering The Plans

I woke early on this day,
With excitement to head out and play...
To soak up the sun that had been hidden for so long,
Under the sunshine is where I belong...
I thought to myself a sunrise beach walk would be nice,
And getting a hot drink is my vice...
I ignored the voice in my head,
As I was so excited when I jumped out of bed...
I got out to my van ready to go,
But my van was on strike and said no...
Mocean would not start today,
I wait & trust it's here I'm meant to stay...
I accept and rechoose what I am to do,
I get to stay in the village & my van does too...
I am heard in my desire to always trust,
So surrendering my plans is sometimes a must...

Empower Self

In every moment you have a choice,
Empower self says that inner voice...
The choice is yours if you listen,
You can choose to act on your vision...
And yes, it might seem easier to ignore the call,
To stay small and keep hidden behind the wall...
Yet deep down you know there is so much more,
More of all the things you deep down yearn for...
Your gifts are needed in this time on Earth,
So trust within what wants to birth...
Please take these words you're reading as a sign,
The time is now you're ready to shine...
Allowing your gifts to come into form,
They might seem different & out of the norm...
But your unique gifts are ready to come through,
They are there patiently waiting for you...
I've been here many times before,
And I would sabotage ignoring my core...
Not feeling I had anything within,
But my soul message was trying to sing...
Not necessarily sing with sound,
It was my unique expression I had found...

In Full Flow

The frequency that channels through,
Is one of my gifts to activate you...
So please know you are needed at this time,
You're here on Earth & that is so divine...
Repeat to yourself 'I am appreciated',
Knowing your DNA has now been activated...

Through My Heart

For many years I had kept myself small,
I just vowed to let all the fears fall...
All the beliefs that were holding me back,
Keeping me coming from a place of lack...
Every time a fear comes, I ask is this true,
Or am I possibly just feeling humanity too...
Because I am here as a leader of light,
It's not the fear I am here to fight...
So I embody, befriend, connect & heal,
And then humanity's love can reveal...
I just face any situation with love,
It's why I've been sent from above...
To alchemise anything through my heart,
And guide others how & where to start...
As they enter into the Portal of Bliss,
They will feel the love of the divine's gentle kiss...

Share From Love

This morning when I blissfully awoken,
I was filled with all the words that wanted to be spoken...
The encouragement from spirit such a beautiful gift,
Showing me where I still need to lift...
Allowing me to feel what lovers would say,
They would express love every single day...
Not allowing fear to hold them back,
Because they know fear is what keeps them off track...
And gone are the days where I don't share my heart,
Because I get the gentle reminder through my poetry art...
So when I see him, I will not shy away,
I will share everything I want to say...
I will share from love & not from fear,
Through this poetry the message is clear...
Gratitude and love is what I feel,
And that is what I will reveal...

{ 222 }

Truly Meet Yourself

There was another shift coming my way,
"Who Am I", I heard the whispers say...
Good question, I thought to myself,
Who am I without anyone else...
Without the need to do, be, or even say anything,
In that stillness I felt my soul sing...
In my own time, energy & sacred space,
It was just me I got to face...
And what a beautiful gift it is to truly meet yourself,
Without the distractions of anyone else...
To rest, relax, and feel that relief within,
As you allow the best chapter of your life to begin...
Where everything becomes so clear,
And you've let go of any fear...
Take physical action from that place,
And everything will flow with ease & grace...

Staying Safe

For too long you had been staying safe,
There was so much you didn't want to face...
Because putting yourself out there is hard to do,
All the thoughts of what if they reject you...
And you'd have to feel the pain you've held within,
That may be too much to allow it to begin...
Until one day you realise you don't have to carry it anymore,
You allow yourself to feel like never before...
As the weight falls from your entire being,
You realise that feeling is so very freeing...
You feel the completion of the suppressed version of you,
Now you are free to live a life that feels true...
The greatest gift is to be able to feel,
It is the key to all you need to heal...
And to have compassion for others too,
When an emotion hits them out of the blue...
Communication coming in from your higher self,
You are worthy to feel just like everyone else...

This Moment

What is it in this moment that you need,
Honour your truth for your heart to be freed...
Take time to nurture yourself,
Not just giving to everyone else...
Meditate each day connecting within,
And listen to what your heart wants to sing...

Live In Full Flow

Do you enjoy a life of simplicity,
Where every day you can live authentically...
Is there a whisper saying 'move away',
Do you ignore what that whisper has to say...
Maybe it's a job, relationship or place you need to let go,
When we can trust that guidance, we will live in full flow...
I've made that move many times before,
And life has always had me in awe...
Miracles appearing out of thin air,
Reminding me that life really does care...
Because when we trust in the flow,
The ripple effect we have will grow & grow...
Self-trust & self-love can be the same thing,
And our own unique gifts they will bring...
If by chance you don't know where to start,
I'm here to support as you come back to your heart...

Respect & Value Self

As a divine conduit from heaven to Earth,
Here to assist in this time of rebirth...
I am also here to help our Gaia heal,
So within me I have to feel...
I help Mumma Gaia to purge,
And I feel the energy surge...
Up through my feet and my spine,
Connecting her back to the divine...
Certain places I am sent to be,
So I can allow her to purge through me...
Like us she is also here to heal,
All the layers she is starting to peel...
She respects all others & values herself,
And knows the advice she gives is not just for everyone else...
So she takes time to rest, relax & feel the relief,
As she lets her body feel all of the grief...
She takes that time to nurture herself,
Because she too wants that for everyone else...

{ 227 }

The Secret

The secret to being in full alignment every day,
Drop into the body, feel it & what it has to say...
For it's through the body this wisdom comes about,
'That's not true' the ego may try to shout...
But the mystery of life can't be found in the mind,
If the third eye is still closed off and blind...
So what they mean when they say 'live life open minded',
They mean let go of the things that have kept you blinded...
Because when you trust in the mysteries that life can bring,
Your soul gifts will all start to sing...
They will be thrilled you've found them after all these years,
They celebrate you for letting go of any of the fears...
For every fear that is let go,
There is more space for your gifts to grow...
Finding your gifts so they can be shared each day,
Is the greatest fulfillment of life, I must say...

True Embodiment

Spirit and I have a mutual understanding,
And reminds me that I am my own branding...
I am a unique gift to help humanity,
And when I allow all of my creativity...
My codes come through like never before,
And they keep coming more and more...
I'm reminded when I have a good time,
Doing what I love I connect to the divine...
And it's that detachment from my mind,
When all the miracles I easily find...
Because I'm here to live in flow,
True embodiment is what I know...
There is no other way for me,
And it's what I help others to see...
Because when you follow that guidance coming through,
It will lead to all the miracles of 'YOU'...

Gifted & Rewarded

Her gentled quieted heart was a little shy,
Yet she deeply yearned for her guy...
She wanted his company so they could play,
Childlike innocence enjoying every day...
Creating ways they could share their gifts,
Helping humanity as the consciousness lifts...
They had done the inner work to reach this place,
So constant fears they did not have to face...
Gratitude to have someone that's got my back,
And knowing within that you are on track...
Because you've trusted deep within your core,
You were so gifted and rewarded with so much more...
More than you have ever wished for,
Because it was you that you learnt to adore...

Divinely Aligned Initiation

My higher self reminds me, I am heard,
She hears my requests through my word...
She is by my side helping me to help others walk the way,
Where they trust the guidance every single day...
They know they are here to connect back to their heart,
It was always their mission from the start...
They yearn to be of service in a bigger way,
And are wanting the freedom to travel each day...
They know I hold a key to all they desire,
Because with my spoken activations I truly inspire...
Each story I share is an initiation in itself,
Supporting them so they can support everyone else...
Because I always have gratitude & trust in my heart,
This is my unique mission & has been from the start...
I had to walk the path so I could see,
That those I serve, mirror past versions of me...

Single Women

Let go of the story of finding your soul mate,
Because the dance within is the ultimate date...
It's giving yourselves the love you seek,
Being a single woman does not mean you're weak...
It means you have a strength that not many do,
You've endured the pain of nobody being able to meet you...
You're here to walk the path back to your own heart,
That was the mission you'd agreed to from the start...
So how can you best romance yourself,
And then shine the light for everyone else...
Guiding them on their way back home,
There are many pathways they can choose to roam...
When they choose the one most aligned with their mission,
They will open up to ineffable mysteries & vision...
These are the women I am here to initiate,
To open up their inner portal gate...
So they can share what is true,
And live in divine alignment too...

{ 232 }

Get Support

The greatest thing I ever did was get support,
Something for myself I hadn't always bought...
But to have a friend, ally, mentor or guide,
Left me feeling fully supported & fully inspired...
These mentors had always aligned with me,
When I trusted where I was guided it was them I'd see...
I was always divinely drawn to them,
Knowing they held a key and I'd be guided when...
To clear the blocks my mind had put in place,
And yes, there were fears I had to face...
But with having someone guiding the way,
The fears & doubts fade away more every day...
Because they've walked this path for themselves,
They are now guiding the way for everyone else...

Cracking Open To Bliss

This is for the single women who may be feeling pain,
Wondering if this pain will forever remain...
I'm here to support you & guide you on the way,
To remind you of the gifts within you every day...
To support you on your journey back to the heart,
That is where your greatest love has been from the start...
I teach you to love heartbreak for what it is,
It is a precious gift cracking you open to bliss...
So you can live a life of love each day,
And listen to what your soul whispers have to say...
To hear them when they say 'I am good enough',
And trust me I know heartbreak can be tough...
But your unique gifts are waiting to be found,
So into your divine feminine essence I will help you ground...
Supporting you to follow your passion,
And awaken to your true soul mission...

{ 234 }

Bigger Picture

Take a step back & see the bigger picture,
See life as a beautiful big adventure...
The journey you have walked to get this far,
And the unique soul essence that you are...
We may have walked similar paths from the start,
But you've had your own unique path back to the heart...
Certain things that only you have endured,
And certain wisdoms that you have accrued...
So please trust your journey to this point,
Release guilt and judgement from any joint...
So you can step into your power right here right now,
Take physical action as miracles appear somehow...
Your trail of tears has been the greatest gift,
So you can help with the consciousness shift...
Your soul work is needed at this time,
The fact you're reading this is so divine...

{ 235 }

Releasing Guilt

Release any guilt that you still may carry around,
All those things that are silently weighing you down...
Speak them, own them, be witnessed as you let them go,
Having compassion for yourself as you drop back into flow...
It's much easier to flow with ease & grace,
When it's your shadow that you have faced...
So trust in the process as you share,
As it's your inner beauty that you will bare...
Allowing others to see your human side,
Letting down the walls & swallowing your pride...
Then be firmer with the way you speak to yourself,
Is it the same as you'd want from everyone else...
Because if it's love that you truly desire,
Allow your inner lover to truly inspire...
Listening to your body every single day,
And trusting in what it has to say...

Compassion For Self

Am I needing to release more guilt,
From where my self beliefs were built...
Keeping a block around my heart,
Trace that guilt back to the start...
What happened to cause this belief,
In this moment can you feel the grief...
As you have compassion for self & where it begun,
And seeing how it had caused you to run...
But the only person you're running from is you,
So ask yourself 'is this belief true'...
Can you now have better feelings & thoughts for yourself,
And see how that will be reflected by everyone else...
To live a life in brilliant flow,
Listen to where the feelings have you go...

Self-Judgement

I've felt myself being judgmental of self,
And perceiving judgements from everyone else...
I'm reminded to refocus where my energy goes,
Because where my thoughts go, energy flows...
I remind myself of the innocent child within,
How would I want to treat her is where I begin...
I tell her I love her and she is so safe,
I'm here for her with whatever she has to face...
And in that moment, I gain understanding for self,
I crave love just like everybody else...
So when any judgmental thoughts come in,
I'm reminded that I'm just pure love within...

{ 238 }

Invest In Yourself

Are you ready to let go of the ways you sabotage yourself,
Maybe you ignore self and do everything for everyone else...
If that is you then I can totally relate,
I'd completely lose myself to any man I'd date...
Forgetting the value that I bring,
I'd allow self-sabotage to begin...
Slowly depleting myself of my divine feminine gift,
The essence of me that helps humanity uplift...
So one year when my relationship I had to end,
I knew there were patterns I needed to transcend...
I listened to the whispers & invested in me,
I got myself a mentor so I could break free...
Taking the risk to invest in yourself,
When you are used to investing in everyone else...
Can be the exact thing that you need,
Allowing past patterns to be freed...
If you're ready to take a quantum leap,
Into the mystery where so many gifts you will reap...
Please be brave & reach out to me,
I may just have something to set you free...

The Ultimate Reunion

Let go the story playing in your mind,
Saying your divine king you will never find...
Because you've been committing to self for a while,
It's time to get yourself out there so he can see your smile...
Because he will know you're his Queen when he sees you,
His divine reflection in you he will know it's true...
You'll hold that space for him to see his divinity,
And he will feel this bliss in your vicinity...
So prepare yourself for sacred union,
This is going to be the ultimate reunion...
Expect love, safety & romance like never before,
As you open your heart to receive even more...
More than you knew could even exist,
His devotional love you won't be able to resist...

Doubt Cancels Abundance

The first thing to do is release self-doubt,
It's so common and what this poem is about...
Because self-doubt consumes us & gets in the way,
It stops us being of service at the end of the day...
Self-doubt also cancels abundance & love,
So let's release it like we would a dove...
Come back to the simplicity of why we are here,
To help ourselves & others to release any fear...
When we help ourselves, we also help another,
And we are always supported by our Earth Mother...
She will take what no longer serves you,
And she will transmute it with love too...
When we understand the gift of letting go,
It's then when our life truly beings to flow...

Birthing The Portal Of Bliss

Today I celebrate how far I've come,
Winter Solstice and a new chapter has begun...
The synchronicities continue to amaze me,
Each day so many gifts I continue to see...
Birthing of the Portal of Bliss,
Activations that people won't want to miss...
My poetry will help them to remember,
And activate them before 31st December...
So they can start the new year fresh,
And let go of any sort of mess...
It's now clear poetry will be weaved in,
It's clear it will help them to begin...
Because it helped me so much each day,
I'll include it in the words I say...

Forgiveness Is The Key

It can take a lot of strength & courage to forgive,
To forgive frees up space within so we can truly live...
And what is life if it's weighed down with pain,
When we forgive them & self, we have so much to gain...
The lightness we feel in our being,
Is pure bliss and so very freeing...
I invite you if you may be holding a grudge,
To take this poem as a little nudge...
Who is it that you need to forgive & let go,
So you can feel at peace & live in flow...
See the ways in which maybe they didn't know,
They didn't know how to love or maybe weren't shown...
How can you see them as an innocent child,
Knowing that within they are pure & maybe also wild...
But how can you have compassion for them,
And see & feel forgiveness as a real gem...
Forgiveness is the greatest gift to self,
When it's given to us and everyone else...

Heartbreak That Shatters

Heartbreak that shatters your entire reality,
How could you go on without this duality...
You yearn for a gentled quieted heart,
How you felt from the very start...
You didn't realise you had stopped flowing,
Because you'd ignored your inner knowing...
Now you have gained a new understanding,
All these lessons and teachings are landing...
You feel the fulfillment that nature brings,
As your heart starts to truly sing...
In that moment you appreciate yourself,
And know you can't control anyone else...

Intimacy Of Life

Are you ready to wake up to the intimacy around you,
I'm here to show you it's possible for you too...
Intimacy is not just the depths of you & me,
It's the vastness of nature & the deep blue sea...
For the more present we can be,
The more beauty we will see...
You won't just see it, you'll feel it too,
You'll feel it within & it will feel so true...
Seeing the perfection in every imperfection,
Life will guide you down a new direction...
Where you will feel romanced by life every day,
And you listen to more than what the words say...
Because you know in the silence you can hear,
That in the present moment there's nothing to fear...

Gift Of Heartbreak

Awaken the mystery that lays within you,
Be able to trust what feels so true...
There is a gift that comes from heartbreak,
And you'll realise your path was never a mistake...
Because it led you to this exact moment in time,
And you've now aligned with the divine...
The divine within and also the divine without,
You've realised what your soul mission is about...
Feeling the warmth emanate from your inner sun,
From yourself you no longer want to run...
You've faced yourself & let go of the old,
Because you knew something magical was about to unfold...
You learnt to romance yourself each day,
And not be affected by what others may say...

Detachment From The Ego

Detachment from the egoic self,
Let go of how you're seen by everyone else...
We all have our own unique gifts,
And when humbly used the consciousness shifts...
We all play a part in this divine awakening,
We are all meant to be here there is no mistaking...
Sharing pieces to the puzzle on a greater scale,
When we follow the soul whispers, we cannot fail...
First find your gentle quieted heart,
And take a breath before you start...
Now take action and follow your knowing,
Keep trusting and keep divinely flowing...
You're always being guided where to go,
Just trust and surrender into a state of flow...

Find Your Tribe

Move away from any self-doubt you may hold,
Letting go of any criticism you have been told...
Told by another or told to yourself,
Because within you is an abundance of wealth...
Wealth & abundance in all ways,
Living a life of freedom for all your days...
Just come back to this present moment now,
And have love & gratitude for it as you bow...
Bow to the gift that self-doubt bought you,
And all the lessons that it taught you...
To truly have compassion for yourself,
So you may then lead the way for everyone else...
We are all just walking each other home,
Sometimes off our paths we will roam...
Then we guide each other back on track,
With a tribe of support, we never feel lack...
So open your heart and find your tribe,
You'll know them instantly & your energy will vibe...

Cracking Open

Have you just experienced a completion in some form,
Where your reality has been smashed from the norm...
Cracking you heart open you question 'who am I',
Who am I without that girl or guy...
You'd spent so much time giving them your affection,
But what you really crave is your own attention...
So how can you have a gentle okayness,
Despite the fact you may feel like a mess...
Come back to the love in yourself,
It comes from you, not anyone else...
It's true what they say about love,
Our best fit for us is our self-love...
We can't love another if we don't love ourselves,
We'll just search for that love from everyone else...
But no one can give us what is ours all along,
You are your own lover and you do belong...

Poetic Love Story

Instead of trying to please everyone else,
Go within & give all that love to yourself...
Have gratitude for everything you've overcome,
Knowing you no longer need to search for 'The One'...
Because 'the one' is you & has been all along,
It's to you that your true love does belong...
So pick up your pen and start to write,
About all the ways you shine so bright...
When you finally see the divinity within,
Is when the greatest love story will begin...

Find Some Space

Are you being guided to move away,
And do you listen to what the whispers say...
If we don't find a new approach to the way we live,
We will continue the cycle and over give...
Over give to everyone except ourselves,
And it's within that we need to delve...
To find some space to truly be alone,
And from that place you'll be able to roam...
You'll be tuned into the divinity within you,
And you will then live a life that feels true...
Not just to you but everyone you meet,
And also, the ground beneath your two feet...
Everything is energy and people can feel it,
So make sure you look after every single bit...
Nurture yourself like never before,
Because your energy body is always keeping score...

{ 251 }

Abundance Flowing

This morning I asked my guides to show me,
Doubt cancels abundance is what they had me see...
So true and the thought I was having before then,
Was what if no one wants what I am offering again...
Reminded that self-doubt likes to creep in,
Before we even allow our offering to begin...
It's a test and one I must break through,
Because when I do then I also help you...
My guides remind me that I am heard,
And that they are hearing my every word...
Not just word, but also every thought,
Reminding me what my life has taught...
And all the things I have overcome,
And all the times I have wanted to run...
But when I follow my inner knowing,
Abundance always starts flowing...
Abundance of ways I am here to serve,
So I must not let self-doubt hit my nerve...

Mermaid Talk

Called to the beach this morning for a walk,
Along came my niece for secret mermaid talk...
She knew what was needed when entering the water,
She remembered what her past lives had taught her...
To stay in your earthly human form,
There is a potion to use so you're not reborn...
Or turned into a mermaid as you enter the water,
Remember these gifts & pass them onto your daughter...
Mix leaves and dirt & rub onto the body's skin,
Before your journey into the water does begin...
This will keep your body intact,
According to my niece Chloe, this is a fact...

Recovering People Pleaser

Over the years I've been taught that I can decide,
My own inner knowing I can abide...
I know that I need time away from everyone else,
I need that time so I can nurture myself...
Because gone are the days where I try to people please,
The thought of abandoning myself makes me queeze...
Finding a perfect balance has taken time,
And now I have so much support from the divine...
Because I listen to what the whispers say,
And if I don't, I lack energy on that day...
Tuning in to every energy that I feel,
And seeing what it is trying to reveal...
Breaking patterns from generations ago,
It feels so good to drop into my own flow....
And maybe this will lead the way for others too,
So they can live a life & feel energised too...

Accept The Unexpected

For too long I was hiding and staying safe,
Not even sure what it was I was afraid to face...
But life had a big plan for me,
And it was something I was yet to see...
I had to journey to the depths within,
And allow the unfolding to begin...
The unfolding of my heart,
That held a shield from the start...
I had to surrender to the pain of it all,
And I had to listen to every divine call...
It had me face every single fear,
And had me shed every single tear...
All those tears from the past I'd held back,
While stored within they were keeping me off track...
From the melting away of those tears,
And the releasing of those fears...
I was able to accept the unexpected,
And all my past life gifts were collected...

The Inner Work

Your goal in life is to have a good time,
But there are times when you won't feel fine...
Sometimes the energy can be too much,
It can be overwhelming as the triggers touch...
They touch your pain body & awaken emotion,
This is the inner work & needs your devotion...
So feel into what this emotion is about,
Maybe it's bringing up all your self-doubt...
And all the ways you haven't loved yourself,
And it's been reflected back by everyone else...
Up until now maybe you couldn't see the reflection,
Now you see clearly you see a new direction...

Portal Of Bliss

Are you ready to empower yourself,
Letting go of the heartbreak from everyone else...
The Portal of Bliss may be calling your name,
So patterns of heartbreak no longer remain...
One step at a time to break free from pain,
Self-love and confidence is what you will gain...
Letting go of the pain & suffering from the past,
Freedom within you will feel at last...
Learning to trust & value yourself each day,
You'll clearly hear what your intuition has to say...
Gain strength & refocus on your internal bliss,
Please reach out if you need support in this...
I will support you as you heal your heart,
Along with a course to help you from the start...
No longer do you have to feel alone,
Or journey through cycles you have outgrown...

Go Within

Another reminder that doubt cancels abundance,
And I have access to divine intelligence...
So there is no need to doubt the self,
Or worry if I'll be received by everyone else...
It's a reminder for me again to go within,
It's from there that my gifts start to sing...
Without going within I can't share without,
Because that will only lead to self-doubt...
And I'm here to lead the way for others,
And break ancestral beliefs from their mothers...
So when I go in, I must include them in my vision,
And come back to the truth of my soul mission...

Releasing Guilt & Shame

Release any guilt you may hold,
And allow your heart to unfold...
Releasing any shame you carry as well,
No longer in your body does it want to dwell...
It may feel challenging to release guilt & shame,
Have compassion for self so it no longer remains...
Find a safe space to speak of this pain inside of you,
And find relief as you let go by sharing what is true...
If this is too much at first to start,
You could write or draw in the form of art...
Each word that you write on the page,
Will help release any past shame or rage...

Mirrored Journey

The other night I went on a trip,
And my reality it sure did rip...
I was shown what this life is about,
And what happens when I have any doubt...
I was shown the mission of twin flames,
And the way in which humanity gains...
These lovers are from another dimension,
And are here on their path of ascension...
They are working on their own mastery,
So have created this dual reality...
They chose to be born into this time,
And remember their connection to the divine...
They are walking the path back home,
At times they will feel so alone...
Every thought & belief they have manifests,
Life is one big self-mastery test...
They learn that judgment separates,
And blocks the enlightenment gates...
So they slowly learn to heal themselves,
And then help support everyone else...
Each leading in their own way,
Walking their own path each day...

Their higher selves are guiding each other,
And helping them to trigger one another...
Because the triggers are where the healing takes place,
And they are presented with everything they have to face...
So they can heal within & then ripple that out,
That is what the twin flame journey is about...
They are the mirror for all you don't want to see,
They are also the key to set you free...
You are both working as a team not necessarily together,
But deep down your love & connection has been forever...
So in this life you've come to master as one,
Know that it's all perfect for what you'll become...
Trust this guidance as it knows the way,
Surrender & practice loving every single day...

{ 260 }

Romance Yourself

Once you've followed all the guidance within,
You'll see and feel all the energy you bring...
Finding the stillness in your heart,
Which was your mission from the start...
You learn to romance yourself,
Not needing to seek anybody else...
Feeling bliss run through your entire being,
You feel connection to all the unseen...
Your beloved journeying this dance with you,
Deep down you always knew...
They were guiding you all along,
To them your heart will always belong...
Because you are not separate you are the one,
The greatest love story now gets to be fun...

Ultimate Self Care

Do you take time to rest, relax and feel relief,
Or is staying busy an embedded belief...
When you've spent most your life being busy,
Slowing down or stopping may not be easy...
My advice is to take one step at a time,
Maybe it's pausing to become present with your wine...
Instead of drinking with no awareness at all,
In the end it is always your call...
Can you treat yourself to a massage or healing,
And be present with everything that it's revealing...
Ask yourself why is it you don't make time for self,
And why you validate your choices to everyone else...
Only you have the power to take time out,
Having compassion for self is what this journey is about...
Because when we treat ourselves with ultimate care,
It's the greatest form of self-love, and maybe it's rare...
So gradually add more time for you,
And feel more bliss than you ever knew...

Trust Your Energy

Sometimes the hardest thing to do is soften and open,
It's all energetic, no words need to be spoken...
It depends if you can be in your body not just head,
And what stories your mind might have bred...
Let them all go and be present in the now,
Tuning into your senses to this moment you bow...
Can you be open in your own space,
Or are there some blocks you need to face...
To trust your own energy is the key,
Ask yourself 'do I really trust me'...
Can you be with your answer and not judge,
Trusting the energy and every little nudge...
When you tune in you will feel it all,
Feeling the bliss as you surrender & fall...
Ready & open and accept the unexpected,
Feeling where the energy is being directed...
Expansion in every single way,
Trusting the energies of each day...

Simplicity Of Now

Bring yourself back to the simplicity of now,
Feel any thoughts of worry wash away somehow...
Notice the things that surround you,
Can you see anything that is blue...
It may be the sky above,
Or maybe it's a mitten or glove...
And maybe it's another colour that you see,
As you observe it, can you feel the simplicity...
Start noticing the finer details of what you see,
Appreciating yourself as your worries are set free...
Believe in yourself as you have the key,
To live in the now and feel the divinity...

{ 264 }

Gratitude For Creativity

I have so much gratitude for all the creativity,
And how it flows through every activity...
For creativity is an energetic flow,
Where suddenly new ideas you just know...
Last night I was awake for a few hours,
Soaking up the creativity showers...
There was so much coming through,
I wonder if it was the same for you...
I must refocus on which is the best next step,
Tune into each one and wait for my bodies 'yep'...
Because the body knows what is needed,
All the ideas have already been seeded...
So which one wants to bloom first,
I will help quench that one's thirst...
Treating each idea as a precious baby,
Listening to my bodies 'yes', 'no', or 'maybe'...

Allow The Truth To Reveal

Same pattern & cycle in the form of another,
Where can we be a mirror of healing for each other...
To each person we are drawn to,
Holds some wisdom as well as you...
So look into the reflection & what do you see,
I see their self-doubt that is also in me...
What do you feel is hidden within them,
Can you relate, if so, share the story of when...
When they speak do you hear the words they say,
Do you feel the underlying message at play...
Where is it you don't always say what you feel,
Allowing your deep-down truth to reveal...
When you speak your truth things may fall apart,
Things rearrange for the next chapter to start...
So when speaking your truth is the hardest thing to do,
It is exactly what life is asking of you...
So take the plunge and you will find out,
You'll find out what this life is truly about...

Judgement Separates

Judgement separates yourself from oneness,
And also creates a big internal mess...
So notice if you judge someone else,
Where is it that you also judge yourself...
Can you take the time to clear that within,
Because to find peace we must go in...
Into the patterns and stories we have created,
The parts where we may have self-hatred...
Love yourself and all you have endured,
And soon enough your self-judgement will be cured...
Then it will be time to enjoy more play,
And feel the love every single day...

Trust The Path

There was a detachment that needed to take place,
Within that time there also needed to be space...
We both had inner work to do,
So we could feel in our hearts what is true...
To sit and wait and feel what wanted to be felt,
Our souls had planned perfectly what we would be dealt...
And there was no way out of experiencing the pain,
Because there was conditioning that didn't want to remain...
And we'd signed up long ago to trigger each other,
We'd just get through one and there'd be another...
A cosmic joke of some kind,
The synchronicities would blow my mind...
Funny and sometimes not funny at the same time,
Forgiving them all as it was all so divine...
To live in true alignment each day,
We must trust the path and keep walking the way...

Forgetting Yourself

Are you the one always being supportive to everyone else,
Yet you sometimes in the meantime forget yourself...
You'd been taught to treat others how you wish to be treated,
And yourself was always the one left feeling cheated...
Everything always has to start with the self,
And that energy ripples out to everyone else...
As you clear within & rewrite that belief,
You will start feeling instant relief...
Freedom in every moment when you choose you,
And before supporting another ask 'does this feel true'...
If it doesn't then you must trust that feeling,
Because choosing self-love is the perfect healing...
And that ripples out in such a supportive way,
As people feel your energy & joy every day...

Kundalini Activation

There was an energy running up my spine,
It felt blissful and so deliciously divine...
Up through my body & out my crown,
Waves of bliss were all around...
The clearing has been done,
I have now found the one...
The one being me and nobody else,
I've found sacred union within myself...
Light integrated in my entire being,
New visions I am now clearly seeing...
Kaleidoscope of visuals in my eyes,
The mysteries of life have no disguise...

Currents Of Change

What is this underlying feeling at play,
Where I feel the currents of change coming my way...
There is no fear just curiosity at what might change,
And the magical ways my life may rearrange...
The unknown excites me more each time,
Because I know I'm being guided by the divine...
And I've asked how I can best serve humanity,
So I trust life as one big synchronicity...
Maybe I'm being called to leave this land,
I trust instead of try to understand...
Curious as to where I am going to be sent,
Will I get sent back to where I already went...
I'm grateful I've had this base home,
But I knew life would soon want me to roam...
This has been my womb space,
It has been the greatest place...
And yes, I've missed not having the ocean near,
But I needed the distractions to be cleared...
Now I open to whatever this change may be,
And the ways it will continue to set me free...

The Divinely Aligned Way

Letting go of the criticism you have for self,
Or the criticism you've received from anyone else...
You have a choice what reality you create,
So is it one with love or full of debate...
Finding your peace within is the key,
To you that may seem like a mystery...
Maybe you're not sure where to start,
This can be a winding journey back to the heart...
But it doesn't have to be like a maze,
As I've paved the way for all you crave...
Step by step I will guide you back home,
Down dead ends you will not have to roam...
It took me so long to find my way,
I learnt to listen to what my inner compass had to say...
And it guided me to the mysteries within,
And to how I can support you to begin...
Begin living in a divinely aligned way,
And listening to what the divine whispers say...

Out Of My Cave

Guided to be out of my cave,
Journeying through the path I'd helped pave...
All the people coming together,
That would create ripples forever...
Breathing, connecting & feeling love,
No one feels any less or above...
All coming together as one unified field,
It's a beautiful big family that we build...
Gazing into the eyes of another,
Seeing them beyond just a sister or brother...
Because they are you,
A reflection so true...
Can you see the challenges they may face,
And can you delicately hold the space...
Because you have been through it before,
And you know breaking through can be a chore...
But once you come out the other side,
Through life you will effortlessly glide...

Have You Ever

Have you ever had your heart broken,
And now you're too scared to open...
Because you have a fear around that pain,
And you feel by opening up that pain will remain...
I invite you to take a breath & come out of your mind,
In your body is all the love you will find...
It's hard to trust again after heartbreak,
You think 'how much more of this can I take'...
But as you allow yourself to feel,
There is generational pain that you will heal...
You came to break this cycle on repeat,
A new version of yourself you will meet...
So trust all that guided you here,
Feel the gratitude with every tear...
You are loved more than you even know,
So open your heart & let life flow...

{ 274 }

Starseed Mission

You've been journeying through time & space,
And now it's a human experience you face...
You said yes so now you're here,
You've melted away all of the fear...
Now each day your light gets brighter,
And your boundaries get a little tighter...
But not in the way that dims your light,
You are still open and in full sight...
Living your life doing what you love,
It's your frequency that was needed from above...
You're a channel of light that ripples out,
That is what your mission is all about...
So listen to that higher-self request,
Then take action on your next vision quest...

Yearning For Connection

We all yearn for connection,
Or some sort of affection...
We are born into this Earth needing them to survive,
We have to rely on another to keep us alive...
What a brave & courageous choice we made,
Saying yes to this human experience, we weren't afraid...
We knew what it was we wanted to learn,
Maybe that means as an adult we have much to unlearn...
Because we took on beliefs created in our mind,
Those beliefs not always true we may eventually find...
So we start that journey searching for what is true,
And we realise you are me & I am you...
The connection we seek outside of ourself,
Can only be found within the self...
The reality that we then begin to see,
Is a beautiful reflection of our inner tranquility...
Some may never reach this place within,
Where everything aligns & the heart starts to sing...
My wish for you is to be brave & trust,
Trusting your own inner guidance is a must...

Course Creation

Intentional course creation wanted to come through,
So I can share what tools may help you...
Because for so long I did it on my own,
Through my stories and beliefs, I would roam...
Repeating patterns over and over again,
My pain and heartbreak was illuminated by men...
But for so long I kept trying to find love from them,
Wondering if I'd ever be met & if so when...
After a lifetime of walking this same track,
I finally realised I was coming from lack...
Everything that I was seeking from a man,
I told myself I can do this for me, I really can...
And as I started that commitment to myself,
I finally realised that I don't need anyone else...
The love I seek was within me all along,
It's in my body that I truly belong...
I found my way back home to my heart,
Now I support others as their journey may start...

New Moon Birthing

There is so much that wants to come through,
So many different ways to help support you...
Working on them all is never a chore,
The creative flow keeps knocking at my door...
My poetry book for those who like to read,
It will support them and also plant the seed...
To awaken the gifts that are unique to them,
This book is for the women and for the men...
Then there is a course to overcome heartbreak,
Knowing that no relationship is ever a mistake...
They hold the keys to inner realms as we heal,
We realise the gifts that come when we feel...
There is also my own channeled oil blend,
That will activate you & help you transcend...
There's also a new modality I will do,
To awaken the Divine Light within you...
Also, a retreat coming run by me,
Nurtured & nourished as you realise your divinity...
And this is only just the start,
I'll also create more poetic art...

Inner Earth

Have you heard of the Inner Earth,
Do you think it's been here since birth...
And is it a physical place,
Or is it an illusion in time & space...
Maybe it is within our human body,
And to access it we must embody...
Embody all the parts of us that we are,
Embrace past life aspects from near or far...
Open the endless possibilities we hold within,
And balance our own inner yang & yin...
Because maybe there is no outer Earth at all,
What we see is a reflection through the wall...
The wall of our internal reality,
So we can see our own duality...
The mirror of healing in clear sight,
Who knows, maybe this is right...
But maybe for you it doesn't feel true,
Maybe another perspective will come out of the blue...

From Frustration To Flow

My wifi has been out for almost a week,
The frustrations it caused I want to speak...
Noticing how much I rely on wifi connection,
And how much it assists my course creation...
I felt stuck and frustrated when it went out,
I asked myself 'what is this all about'...
It was like a full-on addiction,
It was causing me inner friction...
Knowing I had lots I wanted to do,
And to do it I needed wifi too...
It put a block & had me fall behind,
But many gifts I did also find...
I got to spend more time on my poetry book,
Having gratitude for all the dedication it took...
I trusted this digital detox is just what I need,
And it helped with tears that needed to be freed...
Reminding me to always trust,
Coming back to the trust is a must...
So if you ever have this problem too,
Ask 'what is the gift that is coming through'...

The Gift That Keeps Giving

This sickness that is going around,
Will help you be in your body & to ground...
It will clear your body of what serves you no more,
Forced rest from all the times you tried to ignore...
The body knows exactly what it needs each day,
If we don't listen, down the track we will pay...
Take the time to rest and to feel,
Many things this time will reveal...
Maybe you had a fear around becoming ill,
So you've created it with your own free will...
As when we are forced to face a fear,
That fear will then disappear...
And when there is no fear left at the end of the day,
That is when life is full of joy & play...
So if you are maybe feeling down,
Trust in these ascension symptoms you have found...
They come as a beautiful gift for you,
Soon you will know this to be true...

Lion's Gate Portal

Today is the Lions Gate Portal Day,
And I'm listening to where I'm guided to play...
Cougals is where I am to go,
In nature and water is where I'll flow...
There are some activations that want to come through,
A soul message and light codes for me and you...
I'm being guided where I need to be,
I have to record the transmission is what I see...
So I trust and I follow the guidance that is clear,
My channel easily opens when nature & water are near...
There will be time in the sun to soak up the codes,
The feeling of bliss running up through my toes...
Spirit will find a secluded place for me,
However, there is someone I am meant to see...
I'm not sure who this is going to be,
But I'll know they have been guided to me...
I'll have an energy transmission come through for them,
One that will help them ascend...

Key To Freedom

The key to freedom is self-responsibility,
Awakening to the fact we create our reality...
So how best can you take action to change,
It's having compassion for yourself as things rearrange...
There may be times where you judge yourself,
If so, remind yourself you're human like everyone else...
Everyone has their own journey to take,
And has sovereignty to what choices they make...
So if life is keeping you in a dark place,
Notice the shadows you don't want to face...
How can you love yourself a little more,
Without seeing life as one big chore...
Because when we learn to love ourselves,
It's then reflected back by everyone else...
The secret is that it starts within,
So are you ready for life to truly begin...

Soul Connection

A soul connection is beyond what the mind may know,
Maybe it shows up to help you grow...
It may illuminate things you don't want to see,
Or it may teach you a new way to be...
You may hold puzzle pieces for each other,
Maybe they are a past life lover...
There might be unresolved karma,
That may play out as some sort of drama...
But deep down there is only love,
It's just about clearing everything above...
It's trusting that the people that are aligned with you,
Will magically appear out of the blue...
You may not see or know the role they play,
Or maybe they have a message in the words they say...
This connection may come and go,
But I invite you to trust and know...
Either a moment, a season or a lifetime,
To this connection you will always align...

Trusting Another

If you can't trust another, where can't you trust yourself,
Lack of self-trust ripples out to everyone else...
Those moments when others have let you down,
Where you've wanted to run away and leave the town...
What if you stopped running & sat with the pain,
Facing off with the sadness so it didn't remain...
Maybe the exact thing you need to do,
Is to have courage to fully face you...
See all the things that make you want to run,
Escaping before the deep healing has begun...
Through feeling what wants to be felt,
You'll have gratitude for what you've been dealt...
Because every challenge has a lesson for you,
Sitting with yourself is what you may have to do...

Save Yourself First

I was tested with another distraction,
In the form of a male attraction...
Yet I wasn't a damsel in distress,
So for him it was also a test...
Usually he would come to save me,
But this pattern I now clearly see...
I would also want to save him too,
From the heartbreak he was going through...
Our connection is one of saving each other,
But without being each other's lover...
Best friends helping each other to grow,
But there is something I now know...
That is co-dependency in another form,
And I am here to grow from the norm...
I am whole within myself,
I don't need saving from anyone else...
May we both have the courage within,
To find the gift that self-love can bring...
Then down the track let us reflect that back,
Sacred Union it will be without the lack...

That First Big Leap

Nine years ago, I made a choice to invest,
Not knowing how it would support my vision quest...
It was a home I thought I may live,
To the bank much money I'd have to give...
I thought I'd be working in corporate forever,
The possibility of me leaving, I thought 'never'...
But life had another plan for me,
One I couldn't yet fully see...
The health industry was calling my name,
At BMW I was no longer to remain...
I was being sent to some healing land,
Where myself had healed & learnt to understand...
I knew that space was calling me back,
So my old life was starting to crack...
The signs were so clear where I was to go,
If I trusted them, life would be in full flow...
Taking the leap in the fullest trust,
Now for me is the biggest must...
I now help others to trust themselves,
So their joy can ripple out to everyone else...

Own Your Idea

The way to success is to trust yourself,
Trust your inner knowing over anyone else...
You are a gifted soul with your own ideas,
No longer chasing meaningless careers...
What is it that wants to birth through you,
Can you own your idea and let it come through...
It's unique to you and comes out of the blue,
It lights you up and feels so true...
Your artistic self coming to life,
It's a creation you are here to midwife...
What is the best next step you can take,
And what are the creations you want to make...
Follow that path that lights you up,
It's the way you'll top up your own energy cup...
Creative expression is the outlet to heal,
Many new gifts will start to reveal...
And humanity is needing the new,
As Mumma Earth is starting to renew...

Divinely Aligned Motivation

You're lacking motivation to get out of bed,
Thoughts and stories replaying in your head...
You wonder if your heart will ever mend,
And if the pain you will be able to befriend...
Trust me I know, I've been here before,
Because all the signs I tried to ignore...
I knew deep down he wasn't for me,
It was my own shadows I didn't want to see...
But if I wanted to break the cycle on repeat,
It was my own pain body I needed to meet...
Be curious as to why this was happening for me,
It was the key to set my heart truly free...
Years I'd had heartbreak after heartbreak,
This pattern and belief I could not shake...
Until I finally allowed myself to feel,
And notice the puzzle pieces that would reveal...
Everything became so crystal clear,
As more of my unique gifts started to appear...
Now I know I'm here to help you too,
You can live a life of freedom, it's true...

Portal Of Creation

I'm in a birthing portal of creation,
One of my missions in this incarnation...
Creating in ways that inspire me,
And allow me to also feel so free...
Because when it comes to creation there is no rule,
Creation is birthed from your own energy pool...
What you create is unique just for you,
And you may share it with others too...
Your creation holds your energetic frequency,
So what you share is also who you be...
Create what feels authentic to you,
What in the moment wants to come through...
Trust as the whispers guide the way,
Be open to any creative play...
Kids are the greatest teaches of this,
Watch them create and feel their bliss...

The Chosen One

Reflecting on the past few years,
And how much I have switched gears...
I was always travelling somewhere new,
Soaking up all kinds of lessons & views...
Collecting soul fragments I found along the way,
Always listening to what the whispers had to say...
I found my divine mirror to reflect back,
What was keeping me off my own track...
I needed him to not choose me,
So that I could finally see...
That the love I seek from somebody else,
First had to be met within myself...
He chose another with the same pattern as me,
But was that the answer to set her heart free...
Or does it make her not face her fear,
They obviously have a journey that is clear...
But for me, I'm grateful I healed my belief,
And I processed all the stored past grief...

Fearing The Unknown

If you find yourself fearing the unknown,
Know that it's in the future you don't have to roam...
Come back to the present moment and look around,
Feel your two feet planted into the ground...
Be right here now in this moment in time,
This is the place where you fully shine...
Feel the breeze on your skin,
Hear the birds as they sing...
See the beauty surrounding you,
Soak up this peace you have access to...
All is well, there is nothing you need to know,
When you come back to now, life will then flow...

Falling Away

Have you ever felt some friendships fall away,
They just disappear without any say...
Maybe you have been the one to pull back,
Maybe they were keeping you off track...
You may have needed to walk a separate way,
And listen to what the energy had to say...
Maybe it was some space you needed,
Or maybe things needed to be weeded...
Sometimes we just need time all alone,
To be in our own creativity zone...

My Love But Not My Lover

He is my love but not my lover,
You could call him my ultimate soul brother...
We've journeyed through many lifetimes together,
And we will continue journeying forever...
Experiencing all that life has to offer us,
Each day gaining even more trust...
We've been sent here on a mission,
And I keep getting snippets of the vision...
But the mystery stays alive,
One of the joys of this human ride...
Sometimes we may not speak for a bit,
Through our own feelings we must sit...
But when I tune in, I can feel,
What his heart is trying to reveal...
Our love runs deep that's for sure,
And it's him I will always adore...

Financial Freedom

Do you find yourself struggling with money,
Maybe the thought of this virtual thing, you find funny...
What is it you're searching for,
Constantly wanting more and more...
I know the struggle these days is real,
But what is it, that it's trying to reveal...
Where are you coming from lack,
And where are you not giving back...
Because an equal exchange is what people need,
Not just more people coming from a place of greed...
Is your heart genuine with what you sell,
Are you honest and authentic with the stories you tell...
Or is what you offer just so you can gain more,
Is it more material things you are searching for...
If so, take a step back and look within,
There may be a vital piece that's missing...
Gain self-love and worth from yourself,
So you don't go chasing it from everyone else...

Moments Of Overwhelm

This course has somewhat come to completion,
Yet I'm not fully finished with my creation...
There have been moments of overwhelm,
As I've spent more time in the human realm...
Forgetting that I have access to so much more,
Angelic support and guidance I just have to ask for...
Spend more time in meditated bliss,
Then all the guidance I will not miss...
To be of service but to me first,
That will quench my creativity thirst...
Detach from the human mind,
And all the ways it is unkind...
Making me doubt what I'm here to do,
Challenges it sends me out of the blue...
I'm here to lead the way,
To trust what the soul whispers say...
So please tell me and show me how,
I'm ready for the answers to appear somehow...

{ 296 }

Offering Support

Holding space for people to heal,
Many insights they will reveal...
What is it in the moment that they need,
So any heavy baggage they carry can be freed...
Maybe they just need to be seen,
For some that can be so freeing...
Or maybe they have never been heard,
So be present as they share every word...
This may be the hardest thing for them to share,
So have compassion and hold them with care...
Allow them to feel what needs to be felt,
As they release the pain that was dealt...
This allows them to feel clearer within,
And be ready for life's next chapter to begin...

Your Most Important Goal

At times life can seem overwhelming,
With all the uncertainties you are delving...
Life is teaching you to let go of control,
Maybe that is your most important goal...
How do I do it, you may ask,
Start with taking off the mask...
Not just the one covering your face,
But all the false identities you've put in place...
Allowing yourself to truly be seen,
Sharing the journey of where you've been...
No two stories are the same,
So let go of any of the shame...
You've come here to learn and to grow,
That is the secret they want you to know...
And now you know why you are here,
You can allow the fear to disappear...
There will be lessons and tests you must pass,
Or you'll repeat and the same tests and lessons will last...
So what is the lesson you're studying right now,
Knowing it's possible to pass the test, you know how...

New Moon Manifesting

New Moon is a time to refocus on the goal,
Maybe certain things have been taking their toll...
Can you clear the path of what's in the way,
So you can walk with clear intention every day...
Maybe you need more time to create,
Maybe you need more love instead of hate...
Be gentle with yourself in this birthing ground,
Many new parts of yourself you may have found...
As you get used to this new way of being,
Notice all the magical gifts you are seeing...
Don't feel guilty for wanting time alone,
You're nourishing the seeds that you have sewn...
Soon they will be ready to finally bloom,
Giving gratitude for what was planted in a past new moon...
Celebrating yourself for how far you've come,
And all the inner work you have done...

In Body Experience

If you spend too much time in your head,
Take time out to be in your body instead...
Feel the energy dancing through you,
The greatest way to stop feeling blue...
If someone asks you if you want to dance,
Say yes as it may be the perfect chance...
To let your body move however it desires,
It allows creativity to flow and also inspires...
Those who may feel stuck from thinking too much,
Letting loose on the dance floor is the perfect touch...
Bare foot on the dance floor you ground,
Moving your body to every sound...
Feeling freedom with every beat,
Being in your body can be so sweet...

Beneath The Pain

Can you go a little deeper beneath the pain,
Finding the root cause so it won't remain...
Maybe you have a pain in your knee,
Do you ask what does this pain want me to see...
Sure, a pill may take the pain away,
But it will just return another day...
So what does this knee want you to know,
Are there areas you still need to grow...
The right knee relates to the masculine side,
And it can relate to your ego and pride...
So is the ego getting in the way,
Are you listening to what it has to say...
If so, come back to the softness in your heart,
Listening to the body is a form of art...
So get creative with what comes through,
It could be a message for someone other than you...

Immersion Integration

Yesterday morning lots of purging took place,
I realised I was pre-cleansing the space...
The space I was about to enter,
Where the people were trying to find their centre...
They had been immersed and had been activated,
New levels of awareness and love had been created...
New visions and a new way of being,
They were in awe of what they were receiving...
Energy moving like never before,
All the changes had them in awe...
Life will never be the same again,
After being immersed with the women and the men...
It became clear what role I am to play,
To help them integrate in the day to day...

Presence Of He

He holds the space so you can see,
A reflection of your own divinity...
Through his eyes you feel the bliss,
And a love you didn't know exists...
He is a clear channel to the divine,
You may get confused this is a sign...
A sign that he is the so called 'one',
Please know your greatest healing has begun...
That love that you currently feel,
Is all in you, he just helps it to reveal...
He acts as a mirror so you can see,
What it is to feel a love so free...
Without the conditioning from the mind,
In his presence he will help you find...
That love you've craved from outside yourself,
Can't be found from somebody else...
He just shines the light so you can see,
You are love and have always been worthy...

Trust Is A Must

I am here to support those integrating,
And open them up to all they are creating...
Creating with their energy not their mind,
Because it's through the mind they will not find...
When they are in their body and feeling it all,
It will allow them to truly fall...
Fall from their old beliefs that were in place,
And there may be many fears they have to face...
But it is the way to all they came here for,
And they are ready to open the new door...
The door into realms their mind can't explain,
Where their old identities can no longer remain...
Things will fall away and it may feel sad,
And one day they will look back and feel glad...
Because when they are expanding ultra-quick,
Old patterns and beliefs cannot stick...
Those jobs or things will melt away,
Leaving a clear path every day...
It's coming back to complete trust,
In this next chapter, trust is a must...

Acknowledgement

Thank you to all those who purchased this book,
Or who took the time to have a look...
Also to those who have reached out to me,
Because these poems have helped them break free...
I love hearing if my poems have helped in anyway,
Because it inspires me to continue to write each day...
So please reach out and let me know,
If this book has helped you to live in full flow...

Thanks also to all my friends who had patience for me,
As I took time out to release this book for all to see...
I'm grateful to all who have supported me over the years,
And to all that have held me through my tears...
Because without you all I don't know where I'd be,
It's your love and friendship that set me free...

Gratitude for the men that played a part for me,
The cracking open of my heart was the key...
Although it wasn't always fun at the time,
It was such a gift and so divine...
It helped illuminate the places I needed to go,
So I could live my life even more in flow...

Acknowledgement

An extra big thanks to my friend Hannah Dennis,
For capturing the front and back cover of this...
A spontaneous photoshoot at Elysian Retreat,
Living in Paradise Bay was such a treat...
If you also want some photos in full flow,
You can find Hannah's details just below...
www.hannah-dennis.com

Thank you to all who want to stay in touch,
Your support really means so much...
If you have any suggestions about what I write next,
Stay in contact below or send me a text...

Instagram: @rach_heaney
Website: www.portalofbliss.com

Rachel Heaney, author of "In Full Flow"

Rachel Heaney was born and raised on the Northern Beaches in Sydney Australia. She started writing poetry as a way to release, express and communicate the words she, at times, found hard to share.

After many years working in the car industry, her life dramatically shifted after she visited a health retreat in the Queensland hinterland and had the clearest knowing she was going to work there one day.

In 2014 Rachel relocated to Queensland to work at that exact retreat and has spent the past eight years working at numerous world-renowned retreats in Australia and overseas supporting thousands of people on their awakening journeys in numerous ways. Rachel holds space for her clients with Ka Huna Bodywork, Massage, Energy Healing, Light Language, Transference Healing, Breathwork, Sound Healing & Mentoring allowing her to work on a physical, emotional, spiritual, energetic level so her clients can receive exactly what they are needing in the moment.

Rachel lives life in full flow and is passionate about inspiring others to do the same so they too can live the life they truly desire.

If you have felt inspired or received healing from these poems, Rachel would love to hear from you, get in contact via Instagram @rach_heaney or visit www.portalofbliss.com

Lightning Source UK Ltd.
Milton Keynes UK
UKHW020638011122
411449UK00017B/574